THE GODS
NEVER LEFT US

THE GODS
NEVER LEFT US

The Long Awaited Sequel to
the Worldwide Best-Seller
CHARIOTS OF THE GODS

ERICH VON DÄNIKEN

A division of
The Career Press, Inc.
Wayne, N.J.

THE GODS NEVER LEFT US
Typeset by Diana Ghazzawi
Cover design by Howard Grossman/12E Design
Crop circle image by innovari/depositphotos
Meteor show background by Wutip/envato elements
Printed in the U.S.A.

To order this title, please call toll-free 1-800-CAREER-1 (NJ and Canada: 201-848-0310) to order using VISA or MasterCard, or for further information on books from Career Press.

The Career Press, Inc.
12 Parish Drive
Wayne, NJ 07470
www.careerpress.com

Library of Congress Cataloging-in-Publication Data

CIP Data Available Upon Request.

CONTENTS

LETTER TO MY READERS

Dear Reader,

In 1966 I wrote my first book, *Chariots of the Gods.* In the introduction I stated, "Writing this book requires courage—reading it no less so. Because its hypotheses and evidence do not fit into the laboriously constructed mosaic of established conventional wisdom, scholars will put it on the list of those books which it is advisable not to talk about." Meanwhile, 50 years have passed. My introduction from that time still stands today. *The Gods Never Left Us* is most definitely not a compendium of my previous works. In only very few sections do I have to cross-refer to my previous books, but only so that the reader is not left hanging.

That extraterrestrials visited Earth millennia ago and influenced our forebears can be proved. But—and this is the ultimate test of our knowledge—ETs are still at work today. And that concerns us all. Why do they do what they do?

What does an extraterrestrial species gain from observing us rather like we observe ants? What have the aliens actually wanted in the millennia to the present day? Can't they leave us in peace? And why do we make it so difficult for ourselves to accept the existence of extraterrestrials?

That is what this book is about. To create the right mood for the main subject, I will start with a strange short story. The following science fiction story may demonstrate how extra-terrestrials influenced humanity since their existence.

Very warmly yours,
Erich von Däniken

CHAPTER 1

THE GODS NEVER LEFT US

"Apparitions don't exist!" Roger Favre growled defiantly. He refused tenaciously to accept the impossible when quite obviously something strange was going on. Something was no longer quite right. Was his mind playing games with him? His eyes? The first signs of Alzheimer's? Were the usual complaints beginning to affect his 70-year-old body? Roger no longer felt quite sure of himself, but was unwilling to discuss it with anybody. Perhaps a bit less alcohol? Stop smoking? Or should he do what all the know-it-alls were recommending: more exercise? And give himself a heart attack?

Roger Favre sat in the same armchair in which he had been watching television for years. It was heavy, made of dark leather, with a slight bulge to support his neck and wide armrests on both sides. Roger smoked, skimmed through the daily paper, and waited for Madelaine to call him when dinner was ready. This is what had happened every evening since his retirement and nothing seemed capable of shaking this routine until, well, until something was no longer quite right. Until these strange lights started appearing.

Among his acquaintances, Roger was seen as an even-tempered kind of person. Some called him boring, others humorless, but all valued his knowledge of his subject. Roger had worked for decades as a geometry teacher in the town's high school. In French-speaking areas, high school teachers were called "professor." Monsieur le Professeur. If there were questions about measurements or volume, and that happened frequently in the city of Geneva, his former students were happy to consult him. Roger had a 46-year-old son who worked for the last 14 years as a physicist at the Conseil Européen pour la Recherche Nucléair (CERN). This son had the same first name as his father. That is why Roger's wife called him "mon petit Roger." My little Roger. Roger senior had become a triple grandfather through Roger junior. The family had done well, and he should have been able to enjoy his existence as a pensioner without any worries. If only there hadn't been the fluttering and intrusive lights that materialized at irregular intervals at foot-level by his television armchair. Roger's wife's name was Madelaine, but he called her "Didi," his term of endearment, because Madelaine, so he thought, made her sound like a maid and a servant. And every few years, Roger fell prey to some whim. Madelaine called it "his obsessions." They came and went like the seasons or the sudden urges of pregnant woman for a particular food. On one occasion, he had planted 30 palm shoots in his garden in a fit of enthusiasm so that it would make him feel as if he were in the South Pacific. The unexpectedly freezing winter turned his South Pacific into Alaska. Another time, he held forth that every responsible paterfamilias had to ensure that he had a power generator in the house. He acquired a diesel engine and dug an illegal pit in the cellar, which he sealed with asphalt. When the power failed in the whole district, the police moved in. His tank was against the law, they yelled, and was polluting the ground water. It had to be pumped out immediately. The whole house stank of diesel for weeks. Another episode worth mentioning was the one with the tunnel. He needed an escape tunnel to save himself and his loved ones below ground in the event of a disaster, Roger asserted with a deadly serious face. He dug valiantly with crowbars, pickaxes, and shovels for 12 weeks and even employed helpers whom he remunerated generously for their silence. Then the groundwater came flooding into the cellar. Not all of a sudden, but rising day after day. Ever since then, Didi had dismissively called the cellar "Loch Ness."

People thought of Roger as kind and helpful, just a bit eccentric. Sometimes. And now the business with the odd lights on the floor. Was he beginning totally to lose the plot?

For two weeks, there had been these strange goings-on. Roger had bought the daily paper at the kiosk, drank a couple of beers in the Bar du Léman, and when he got home, greeted Didi in the kitchen. Like every evening, he had thrown himself into his ancient leather armchair and waited for Didi's call to dinner. As he was leafing through the paper, he was suddenly irritated by a flickering light by his left foot. It was probably some reflection from outside, and then it disappeared as quickly as it had come.

Then it reappeared. Twice. Three times. Where did the
light come from? Roger went to the window, his eyes searched
the street up and down for a car headlight, a reflective piece
of material, children playing with flashlights, anything that
had not been there on previous evenings. He registered no
changes; furthermore, it was the middle of March and the
sun had sunk below the horizon.

Irritated, Roger returned to his armchair. Was he seeing
things that did not exist? Was it his brain? Were his eyes
playing tricks on him? He stared at his shoes. At that moment, it happened again. A knot of colors formed above the
tip of his left foot and arranged itself into a rectangle. Roger
pulled his shoe away; the colors remained, floating about 30
centimeters above the floor. Roger pushed his shoe back into
them. The rectangle of light remained unchanged. Roger
went to the wall and turned up all the light switches. The
lights in the living room shone brightly. Roger knelt down
and felt the carpet, pushing with both hands. The funny light
had meanwhile collapsed, just like when a screen is switched
off.

Roger went to the kitchen and asked Didi for a flashlight.
Didi always knew where everything was. "Are you looking for something in Loch Ness?" she asked mischievously.
"Nonsense," he lied, "I dropped a tablet on the floor." Roger
examined the walls with a flashlight centimeter by centimeter. Somewhere there had to be something reflective. A
microscopic piece of glass? A small glass marble? A picture
frame? The metal wrist strap of a watch? A key? A shiny case

of some kind? A coin? A disk? Was he going mad? "Keep calm," he said to reassure himself. "I'll solve this problem with scientific rigor."

After dinner, he was back in his ancient leather armchair. Roger was actually hoping that the apparition would return. Someone on television was just explaining that the "world wide web" owed its origins to CERN. A certain Monsieur Tim Berners-Lee had developed the "www" in 1989 as a by-product so that scientists could quickly share their research results. Roger thought about phoning Roger junior to tell him about the ghosts in his house. But Roger needed evidence if he was to impress his physicist son. Something concrete. But there wasn't anything. The advertising had come up on the television. Some company was presenting its latest camera. Camera? Roger went to see Didi. She was sitting in the next room laughing about some daft comedy series.

"Didi," Roger interrupted her, "do you know where my old photographic equipment is? You know, the black Nikon bags?"

Didi turned down the volume. "What do you want in the middle of the night with your cameras? Everything is digital today. You can't even find the films for them anymore."

"Does that mean you got rid of them?"

"I wanted to some years ago. But then I hung the little case in the closet at the top of the stairs. The stairs to Loch Ness."

"Thank you," Roger exclaimed. "Perhaps we might be able to sell this old equipment."

Two camera bodies with several lenses were lying in the bag. Exceptional quality. Trigger, settings, self-timer, everything was working as well as ever. The only thing that was missing was film.

The next day Roger went to the camera shop in the Rue du Mont-Blanc.

"Tell me, Jean-Claude, do these old types of film still exist? They were called Kodak?"

"We have them here. This is Geneva—you won't believe the ancient cameras that some UN delegates still like to use."

The two of them sat down over a coffee in the back room. They had known one another since school. Roger wanted to know how a motion-activated camera works. How does a camera only take a picture when something moves?

"You know these plugs, don't you? They send out a weak beam and as soon as something moves in the room the beam is broken and the signal is triggered. The light goes on.

"Can such a system also be rigged up with a camera? I point the lens at a certain spot and set the self-timer. When the light in the room changes, is the picture taken?"

The next day Roger fixed his Nikon to a stool. It had been loaded with a highly sensitive 400 ASA film and connected up to the motion-sensitive plug. Puzzled, Didi enquired, "What obsession is this? We have neither cockroaches nor bugs in our living room."

"I want to find something out," Roger spluttered, and that was indeed true. "My camera is connected to a motion detector which measures the light in the room."

"To what end?" Didi narrowed her eyes.

"I sometimes have problems. Things appear too bright or too dark. Perhaps I need to go and see an optician. This set-up here measures brightness."

Didi shook her head. Leave him be, she thought; this obsession will pass like all the others.

For two days, nothing happened. No apparition in the house. Whenever Roger sat in his armchair, he unplugged the motion detector and disarmed the camera. He placed them on the chair next to him. It was maddening. No lights taunted him. Then, finally, on the evening of March 28, the flickering started again. Roger grabbed the Nikon, put it to his eye, and pressed the shutter release 36 times. It was not possible to use the flash because it would have drowned out the light on the floor. Three days later he held the color photos in his hands and rejoiced. Incredible! Unbelievable! The pictures clearly and unambiguously showed a spot, which grew into a ball of lights. Then a cube formed and finally a colorful rectangle with stripes. While he was taking the photos, Roger had been quick-thinking enough to push his shoe into the picture. It too was recognizable in three pictures in which the rectangle of light was positioned over the tip of the shoe.

"Roger," Roger asked his son on the phone, "can you spare a minute to see your old dad?"

"A bit difficult at the moment. We have more than 60 colleagues from all over the world here. You can't imagine the shop talk. And then there are swarms of intrusive journalists."

"The papers are full of stuff about some elementary particle. What are you looking for?"

"The Higgs boson. Oh Dad! The story is too long to tell over the phone. But you're quick on the uptake. In 1964, the British physicist Peter Higgs developed a theory according to which initially massless particles suddenly acquire mass against the background of the so-called 'Higgs field.' These strange particles explain a whole lot, if we can find them."

"How far have you got?"

"We first started up our particle accelerator last December, then again in February of this year, and currently we are starting the third phase. It all looks very promising. But don't ask about the quantities of energy we need! Almost impossible for the man in the street to comprehend...."

Roger senior knew that. The Large Electron-Positron Collider (LEP) had been brought on stream at CERN as long ago as 1989. When fully operational, this monster gobbled up 100 GeV (gigaelectron volts), the energy used by 10 cities. Now the Large Hadron Collider (LHC) was running, the largest particle accelerator in the world. Roger knew about it from the papers. The accelerator ring had a circumference of about 27 kilometers. It was located directly under the French and Swiss border areas near Geneva, which was about 60 meters underground only a few kilometers away from Roger's house. In this ring—actually a circular tube—9,300 gigantic magnets ensured that the elementary particles, which were accelerated to near the speed of light, did not crash into the wall, but kept to the middle of the tube at incredible speeds. CERN was financed by 21 states and each participant sent their best physicists to Geneva. The public rarely found out what was actually happening at CERN. Not for any reasons of secrecy, CERN was happy to communicate, but because of the complexity of the subject. Particle physics was not popular and not something that could be explained in a few words.

"And when do you expect a breakthrough?" Roger senior enquired of Roger junior.

"That's not so easy to predict. Actually, we are hoping for something in the next few weeks, but anything is possible: a revolution in particle physics or a disaster. You'll hear about it on all channels if we have a successful breakthrough."

"Just one more quick question, son, before you go," Roger said. "I've heard some stupid rumors. Is what you do actually dangerous? I read recently that some physicists had warned that you could produce a mini black hole that could swallow up the whole world. After all, the popular media often refer to this Higgs thing as the 'God particle.'"

"Dad, you really don't need to worry about anything. I and many other of my colleagues know the calculations. Nowhere can a black hole come about. That would require a million times the energy we have now. When all the fuss here is over, I look forward to coming home for a meal. Bye! Love to Mum! I'll be in touch!"

Roger put his cell phone aside and looked thoughtfully at his 36 color photos. He picked up one photo after the other. And his suspicion kept growing. Was the rectangle of light in his living room connected with the experiments conducted with the Large Hadron Collider? Was something uncanny manifesting in his house that might be of burning interest to the physicists at CERN? Troubled, Roger wanted to phone his son again but thought better of it. He needed more evidence, better photos. Pictures from another angle.

So Roger obtained a batch of very fast Kodak film, everything Jean-Claude had in stock. The living room turned into a hunting ground. Roger no longer sat in his ancient leather armchair, but propelled himself across the carpet on a small chair with wheels he had acquired from a home for the elderly. He had his camera round his neck as if he were out stalking. Both cameras were loaded, and he had four different lenses available.

Didi became concerned. "Can you really not explain to me what all this is about? You're behaving like normal, but I know your eyes and your impulses."

Roger took her to one side and attempted to explain to her something about the Higgs particle. He showed her the 36 pictures.

Didi looked nervous. Uncertain, she said, "And there is nothing that will explode? You don't have any chemicals in the house?"

"No, my darling. Not even a Bengal Match."

Didi stared at the floor, then back to the 36 pictures lying spread all over the small table.

"We have to inform our son," she said defiantly.

"Already done!" Roger affirmed. "The physicists at CERN are all busy with this extraordinary experiment. They are looking for the non-existent elementary particle. As soon as the flurry of activity is over, your little Roger will come for dinner."

In the next two weeks, the rectangular light appeared at various times of the day. Roger took photos from all angles: from the front, both sides, the back, and from on top with and without the lights on in the room. What on Earth...? It couldn't be a Higgs particle. As far as he knew, the particle disappeared as fast as it appeared. It decayed into other elementary particles—transformed itself. Roger had read up on it. As a result, he had learned that this Higgs boson corresponds to a quantum excitation of the Higgs field—whatever that was—at any rate, not something that remained stationary in the air and allowed itself to be photographed from all sides. But still: the light field existed. Roger could prove it as clear as day with 234 pictures. Roger junior would be in for a surprise. Full of excitement, Roger waited for the call from his son.

May had come. Mild weather on Lake Geneva. The icy tips of the French Alps sparkled in the distance. On the southern slope of a hill 800 meters distant from the runway of Geneva airport sat two generations of the Favre family under a wide sun shade. Roger had cracked open the first bottle of champagne.

"We've done it," Roger junior reported proudly and nodded with a laugh. "Dad, none of this must get out. We've discovered the Higgs particle. Definitively and for all eternity. It's incredible. Old Peter Higgs was also there. He cried with happiness; we all held hands and danced around in a circle. A unique moment! Twenty-six particle physicists behaving like children. But we decided only to go public with it in a few weeks. Our results have to be documented squeaky clean. So that journalist can also communicate them."

"Congratulations! You're wonderful!" Didi raised her glass to her son. "Are we about to become the parents of a Nobel Prize winner?"

"Mum, you're letting your imagination run away with you. We are a large international team. The honor is due to Peter Higgs. He calculated the particle in advance."

The three of them fell silent. Roger turned to his son.

"Do you have time to listen to an unusual story?"

"From you, yes!" Roger junior laughed and raised his glass again.

An hour later, he knew everything. He had looked through the photos again and again. He had trekked with his Dad into the living room, had sat down in the ancient leather armchair precisely at the moment that the apparition reappeared. Now Roger junior had become an eye-witness— an experience that embedded itself in his brain cells in precisely the same way as the discovery of the Higgs boson. The men debated how to proceed. The physicist Roger said to the geometry professor Roger, "This is too crazy for me to get anywhere officially in CERN. I know two really good guys, both particle physicists like myself and both up for a joke. With your permission, Mum, Dad, I'll invite them here. Saturday perhaps?"

The one physicist was a man called Zwicky from the Swiss canton of Glarus, and the other, who looked like a gym teacher, was from Clermont-Ferrand in France and called Durand. They had a good sense of humor and started by telling jokes from the academic world.

After the jokes, things turned serious. Roger told his colleagues about the events in his Dad's house. He showed them the pictures and, champagne glasses in hand, they all went into the living room where, as if by command, the colored field lit up. It had rarely been gone in the last few days and had, indeed, grown a little, rather like someone zooming in on an image. Mr. Zwicky and Monsieur Durand admired the colorful patterns from all sides. They wanted to be sure that they were not seeing a reflection of some kind. They placed newspaper around the light patterns so that any reflection, no matter from which angle, was impossible. Then the deliberations started. Theories, speculation, and mad ideas were discussed and discarded again. Mr. Zwicky said that he had particularly noticed the irregular colors. The thing was displaying a different pattern from the front than the back. The back part was not a copy, not the front side shining through.

"Perhaps the whole thing is a hologram. Three-dimensions, and we're only seeing two sides. Like the first and last page of a book. But the part in between is missing."

The men decided to conducts some experiments. They would bring some highly sensitive detectors to try and detect the source, the origin of the light.

Two days later, the living room was turning into a laboratory. Small boxes were attached to metal racks bought in a DIY store. Lasers shone in a variety of colors from one rack to another. They touched the mysterious rectangle of light 30 centimeters above the ground. The set-up of the experiment was changed several times. Four hours later, Monsieur Durand was exasperated and close to giving up. "That thing is not shining from anywhere. It does not have a source— somewhere behind the wall, on the ceiling or from outside. The color image is being created directly at the site where it is flickering right now."

The clearly brilliant Mr. Zwicky from Glarus thought they should try and find the "message." There was a message there, wherever it might come from, and the key was to make it visible. The three physicists connected a laptop to several of the devices. An invisible laser beam—this, too, was something Roger had not come across before—scanned the very thin lines at the side of the square. The lateral side of a piece of paper, as it were.

Suddenly complete silence fell. Breathlessly, they all stared at the screen. Binary code began to form in five blocks:

00110001 00110010 00110001 00110110 00110010 00110001 00110001 00111000

00110001 00110010 00110010 00110010 00110010 00110001 00110001 00111000

00110000 00110001 00110000 00111000 00110010 00110001 00110001 00111001

00110000 00110001 00110001 00110100 00110010 00110001 00110001 00111001

00110000 00110101 00110000 00110101 00110010 00110001 00110001 00111001

"Where have these numbers come from?" Roger junior whispered in astonishment. "Or is someone winding us up? Are we in something like the TV program 'Hidden Camera'?"

"Shush!" Mr. Zwicky said, annoyed. "I'm just trying to make the code readable! Here—look!"

12162118

12222118

01082119

01142119

05052119

All of them stared at the small laptop screen. Thoughtfully Mr. Zwicky explained, "It makes sense: The first two lines of numbers end with "2118," the next three with "2119." So they're calendar dates written in the American style. That is, first the month, then the day, and finally the year. Here in Europe we'd write it like this:

16 December 2118 (12.16.2118)

22 December 2118

8 January 2119

14 January 2119

5 May 2119"

"Yes and...? *Who...*?"

"No idea." Zwicky and Durand looked at one another perplexed. Then they all gathered around the table. The dates pointed to the future. Today's date was May 5, 2012. The first date on the screen was December 16, 2118, seven months and 100 years in the future. What was going on here? Again and again the group of men checked whether they were not falling for an outright prank. Maybe their colleagues from CERN thought something up to hoax them.

The next idea came from Roger junior: "Is there any possibility of responding on the same frequency? When someone sends me a message, I can send a response...."

"In theory, yes," said Durand pensively. "What should we tell the sender?"

Mr. Zwicky had already started. He typed the date, "May 5, 2012," on the keyboard and followed it up with "Who are you?" He wrote all of this in English and in binary code because the group of physicists assumed that this was the language everyone would understand.

With these keystrokes darkness descended. Not just the screen on the laptop, but the strange light box 30 centimeters above the floor as well. It seemed as if their message had arrived somewhere. Nothing further happened for the rest of the evening. Peter Zwicky—by now they were all on first-name terms—tried to send a further two messages. But the link had gone. Were they all caught in a common dream? Victims of unknown mind control? Reality seemed to have gone out the window. Objectively, Peter noted that everything was real and could turn out to be important. It appeared that their unknown partners somewhere out there had possibilities at their disposal, which they were lacking.

"And that means that there is no explanation other than that the strangers are coming from the future. They'll be back in contact—if they want to."

The group continued their discussions into the early hours of the morning. Roger, the geometry professor, insisted that nothing could come out of the future. Nothing whatsoever. And that included messages. Period. Jacques Durand referred to the Swedish physicist Max Tegmark. In scientific journals, he had postulated parallel worlds, universes existing alongside ours without us noticing. "Little Roger" referred to the work of the mathematician Kurt Goedel, who had said decades ago that Einstein's general theory of relativity allowed for tears in space and time. And messages? How was that supposed to work?

"Imagine a very finely meshed net on a tennis racquet," Zwicky explained. "When the tennis ball hits the racquet it makes an indentation. The space becomes curved. Now imagine a tiny but extremely heavy ball in place of the tennis ball. It will curve the net to such an extent that it closes into a sphere which completely surrounds the tiny ball. The microscopic but very heavy ball would be the time machine. It could leave the sphere in any place. That, by the way, results from Einstein's general theory of relativity—but you know that. The incomprehensible part is that the time machine lands in a different dimension when it leaves the sphere because there are an infinite number of dimensions around the space. Pictorially, there are a trillion other spaces next to the space in which we happen to be at this moment only a fraction of a nanomillimeter away from us.... Quantum physics makes the most impossible things possible."

"Mumbo jumbo as well?" someone asked.

"Quantum physics *is* like mumbo jumbo," Mr. Zwicky remarked calmly. "According to the tachyon theory of our revered colleague Gerald Feinberg, cause and effect can even be reversed...."

As morning arrived, the men took a taxi home. The apparition did not return until the day after.

Peter had connected the laptop to the printer. A very clear 3D image glinted on the screen. Everyone could recognize the slightly bent banana shape of Lake Geneva from above. And around it was the city of Geneva, only much bigger than in 2012. An expanse of houses intersected by wide roads surrounded both sides of the lake. On the left, it extended as far as today's Swiss city of Lausanne, on the right side opposite, as far as the spa town of Evian in France. And above the picture there fluttered the unmistakable blue flag of the UN.

"I don't believe it!" Jacques remarked derisively. "Simply impossible! If that image comes from the future there would still have to be a UN in 106 years' time and its flag would also have remained the same as today. That can't be!"

"What could we ask them?" Peter Zwicky interjected thoughtfully. They agreed on the sentence "Please identify yourselves."

The response came by return: "We are the descendants. We are experimenting with bridging. According to the old Christian calendar, today is May 7, 2119."

"Ha! Insane!" Peter scoffed ironically. They say they're in 2119—just like that!"

"Slowly I'm beginning to believe in the impossible," Roger remarked. "Just think of the benefit we can obtain from knowledge out of the future. They're more than a hundred years ahead of us! Their knowledge will reduce the time needed for our research...."

"...and our research budgets..."

Until then, the only proper smoker among the four physicists has been Roger senior. Now everyone was puffing nervously on their cigarettes. It was clear to all of them: They had to inform their colleagues and bosses. The discovery of the "Higgs bosons" was small beer in comparison to a dialogue with the future. The consequences were unthinkable!

Together they agreed to ask their partners in the future a question: "Albert Einstein calculated gravitational waves and postulated that these waves would cause the curvature of space. Has this theory been proven?"

There was no response. The connection was broken off from the other side. The screen remained dark. That is why neither Roger junior nor senior, neither Peter Zwicky nor Jacques Durand, informed their colleagues. Peter said what all of them were thinking. No knowledge was allowed to reach the past from the future. It would change the future.

The men agreed to give up the research laboratory in Roger's living room and dismantle the devices, lasers, and racks in the living room. But then the screen lit up again. Eight people with faces of almost supernatural beauty revealed themselves. Each one had the same large eyes, the same regular slightly smiling lips. Each one was wearing a kind of dark blue overall and each one waved with slow, graceful movements. On the lower edge of the screen the words appeared with a mercurial luminescence: THE FUTURE HAPPENS REGARDLESS. Thinking quickly, Peter started the printer. The pictures appeared in color and with razor sharpness. After two minutes the connection terminated.

The photocopies made by Roger Favre went through several hands. And the world no longer made sense to the small number of initiates of 2012. *Those* were our descendants? All of them very beautiful? Graceful, gentle, no distinction between the sexes? Furthermore, they emitted something alien. Our descendants, extraterrestrials?

CHAPTER 2

CONTRADICTIONS?

Just a few words by way of introduction:

Many millennia ago, when our ancestors were living in the Stone Age, a giant mother spaceship was circling our planet. Smaller shuttles went down to Earth. The group of ETs acted like ethnologists. They studied some tribes, diligently learned the languages, gave human beings tips and instructions for a regulated future, and finally took leave again with the promise to return in the far distant future. This became the starting point for religions on Earth. Our ancestors had classed the strangers as "gods."

These thoughts are not speculation, no kind of hypothesis, or any other kind of theory—they can be proven. Everyone who takes the trouble to study the material reaches the same conclusion. Those who want to, know about it.

The consequences of that prehistoric visit affect all of us: our religions, political systems, ideologies, what we are as "human beings," and our present as much as our future. As an insider, as an "old hand" and author of 40 books on the subject, I am just as familiar with the unanswered questions as the critics are. For the latter, the contradictions appear obvious, problematic, and insurmountable. For those in the know, everything has its compelling logic, including those things that appear to be impossible.

Are there extraterrestrials at all? What do they look like? Why do they look like human beings? What technology enabled them to bridge the light years? What did they actually want here? Why, given the billions of available planets, did they come just here to Earth? And why did they do so precisely at this point in the course of earthly evolution? Why did they leave their home? What do the ETs gain from contact with us? Do they want to exploit us? Why don't they kill humanity off? And why don't they reveal themselves to the general public? Why play games of hide-and-seek?

These are all justified questions. And to each one—without exception!—there is a logical answer. In the meantime, the ETs have started influencing human beings again. I contend that the extraterrestrials were not only here millennia ago, they are here again. They are now and have been for decades. Earth is being observed, studied, and analyzed, and there is contact between the ETs and individual groups of people. Totally insane?

"I am certain about this: sometimes totally unfamiliar objects pass soundlessly through our airspace, displaying flight characteristics which we cannot imitate with the technical means at our disposal."[1]

—Denis Letty, French Air Force Major General and recipient of the Order of the Legion of Honor

"I was a first lieutenant at the Malmstrom air force base in Montana, U.S.A. on 24 March 1967. A UFO hovering above the base had deactivated 10 intercontinental missiles. They all became inoperative."[2]

—First Lieutenant Robert Salas, April 2015 lecture in Sindelfingen town hall

"During my time as an air force attaché in England, I came to the conclusion that something was happening in the skies of our world about which we had no idea.... In general I am convinced that UFOs exist and are a reality."[3]

—Ricardo Bermudez Sanhueza, retired General of the Chilean Air Force und director of the Technical College for Aeronautics

"No institution has the right to block disputes... And that includes the study of unidentified flying objects."[4]

—José Carlos Pereira, Commander-in-Chief of the Brazilian Air Force

"On the evening of March 3, 1997, during my second term of office as governor of Arizona, I experienced something between 8pm and 8:30pm which was contrary to all logic and called my view of the world into question: a huge delta-shaped aircraft flying soundlessly over Squaw Peak in the Phoenix Mountain Preserve. It wasn't an apparition but an enormous solid body whose distinctive leading edge was lined with spotlights and which was crossing the skies across Arizona. As a pilot and former air force officer, I can say with certainty that there was no similarity with any object built by human hand familiar to me."[5]

—Fife Symington III, Republican Governor of Arizona from 1991 to 1997

"At least four different species of aliens have been visiting earth for thousands of years.... Some of the extraterrestrials look like us and could walk down the street without anyone noticing."[6]

—Paul Theodor Hellyer, former Defense Minister of Canada and 22-year member of the Canadian cabinet

"There is no longer any doubt about the objective reality of undefined aerial phenomena, better known as UFOs.... The climate of mistrust and disinformation, not to mention ridicule, displays a surprising form of intellectual blindness."[7]

—Yves Sillard, former Director General of the French Aerospace Agency CNES

"We are participants in a universe which is teeming with intelligent forms of life from which we have cut ourselves off."[8]

—Professor John Mack, Harvard University

"We already have the possibility of flying to the stars.... Whatever you can imagine, we know how it works.... We have the technology to bring ET home. No, it will not require a lifetime to do it. We know how it works. We could have the opportunity to fly to the stars."[9]

—Dr. Benjamin Robert Rich, U.S. aircraft designer and Second Director of the Lockheed Skunk Works, California, 1975–1991. (Skunk Works is Lockheed's secret research department. The stealth bomber was developed there. This statement was made on March 23, 1993, at the School of Engineering Alumni Association.)

"I and some others had the privilege to be officially informed that our planet has already been visited by extraterrestrials and that the UFO phenomenon is real."[10]

—Dr. Edgar Dean Mitchell, U.S. astronaut, Captain of Apollo 14, and sixth human being on the moon

"There is hardly any doubt that some unidentified flying objects are real, three-dimensional, massive objects, existing physically and observable. Their material nature is proven in that they have been logged by various sensor systems."[11]

—Colonel Dr. John B. Alexander, former project leader at Los Alamos National Laboratory and the National Research Council.

With this selection of quotes (there are hundreds more!), it should have become clear even to the most skeptical of skeptics: we are no longer alone. We might not like it; we might want to scream, curse, repress it, refuse to acknowledge it, complain about it, whine, or let our jaw drop; we are no longer alone. Science and rational people will probably look for alternatives, for "logical" explanations in order to categorize the impossible. This is of no use; we are no longer alone. Every one of the witnesses quoted above is a person aware of their responsibilities and each one knows why they said something.

Why did these men do what they did? They want to protect humankind from a shock. They want to introduce the new findings gradually to society. And some of these courageous personalities know more than they are saying because they have had dialogue with the extraterrestrials and have asked them about their reasons. They wanted to know why the aliens have not assailed us despite their technical superiority, why they did not reveal themselves over a sold-out football match, and why they have any understanding for us humans. After all, we don't display any understanding for a colony of ants.

I do not intend to discuss (again!) the general question as to whether or not there is extraterrestrial life at all. Every reasonable person knows we are not alone in the universe. Furthermore, it may be swarming with unimagined life forms, but also with life forms similar to humans. This idea arises from the "panspermia" theory of the Swedish Nobel Prize winner Svante Arrhenius (1859–1927). I have already written about it.[12] And Earth-like planets? Not too hot and not too cold? NASA calculates that there are 4.5 billion such worlds in our Milky Way alone. (Extrapolations from measurements of the Kepler space telescope expand to 17 billion Earth-like planets.)

What do the aliens want here? How do they know about our world at all? We are their scions. The gods created human beings in their image.

Sudden, unannounced contact between ETs and our society would be a disaster primarily for us, but possibly also for the aliens. A science author writing under the pseudonym Claudio Stella says in this respect, "If the probable consequences of contact are war between states, if it therefore leads to death and destruction, there is a lot to be said for not establishing contact."[13]

Why should the ETs be bothered at all about what happens on Earth? What concern of theirs are wars between humans, human feelings, behavior, politics, and religions? The counter-question is, what benefit would extraterrestrials have from a broken Earth, from billions of dead, from destroyed industries?

The answer is our raw materials! Ha! An extraterrestrial species would not mine its minerals, ores, and gold on an inhabited planet. Raw materials are available for free, without war and death, on the uninhabited planets of every solar system, in ours, on the moon, Mars, and not to mention the asteroid belt between Mars and Jupiter. There—on the mini planet Ceres, for example—the raw materials are available in pure form. Robots can mine them without the presence of disruptive life forms, without horrible thunderclouds, and without payment. Why should ETs go in for a war on Earth, make themselves hated, and have to deal with acts of sabotage even after a victory, when it can be done much more simply? The extraterrestrials were never concerned with raw materials. Every solar system is full of them.

Why, then, is there no direct contact with us? Steady on. There are, in fact, connections with individual groups on Earth; I will get to that. But what is absent is the global presence, the impressive, awe-inspiring public appearance.

With whom should the ETs sit down? With the despot of an underdeveloped state who only thinks of their own advantage and does not understand anything about science and technology? With the corrupt rulers of developing countries? What would be the benefit of such contact for the ETs? No contact, then, with fools, but with the leaders of a progressive, technological society. On Earth with the Americans? The Russians? The French or Chinese? Every nation contacted would immediately try to draw some benefit for itself from the information obtained from the extraterrestrials. It would want to gain an advantage over the others. This is the breeding ground of jealousy about the technical superiority of the other and fear of possible subjugation. So should the extraterrestrials reveal themselves to all nations at the same time? Circle around the globe in huge spaceships and appear over golf courses and Olympic stadiums? Plug themselves into the global TV network?

Our reaction would be terrible.

The Pope would announce that the ETs were the Devil's spawn, the Antichrist, and we Christians must never listen to them. The aliens have come to exploit us, to enslave and destroy us, as had already been proclaimed by the Apostle John in his Apocalypse. Things would be no better with the Grand Mufti in Islam or the Chief Rabbi in Jerusalem. The visit of the extraterrestrials would cause all the princes of the different religions to lose their power. A careless word from an ET, for example, that God did not have a son or that there was no original sin and thus no reason for Christ to have died on the Cross, would transform the belief in Christianity into a madhouse.

An extraterrestrial explains in a TV interview that Mohammed, the founder of Islam, did not write a single word of the Koran himself. He had been uneducated and illiterate and all the verses of the Koran had been invented by scholars at a later time. As a consequence, millions of devout Muslims would be lost. A life of prayer, suffering, and hard work for a lie? Life would have lost its meaning.

In Jerusalem, an extraterrestrial with a friendly smile explains to his Jewish interviewer that the God of the Torah who spoke to Moses, who had descended to the holy mountain in fire and brimstone, had only been an extraterrestrial, one of their ancestors who had visited Earth thousands of years ago. Yahweh an ET? A religion, exceptionally well sold for thousands of years, nothing but intellectual nonsense? Based on a misunderstanding of technically illiterate forebears? That cannot be serious! The God of the Old Testament an extraterrestrial? The Jewish community misled for over 5,000 years?

In a debate with the participation of ETs, an anthropologist insists that evolution was a secure part of the scientific worldview. But the ET on the panel explains, "Evolution, yes—but there's more. Earth never was a closed system. Our forebears intervened in the human genome on several occasions." For the Darwinists on Earth, and this really applies to the whole of the academic world, a scientifically well-founded building collapses. Are none of the things true that we human beings have acquired through hard and thorough work? The physicist comments that Albert Einstein had calculated as clear as daylight that nothing was faster than the speed of light. Faster was impossible because when the speed of light is reached mass becomes infinite. But the amiable ET next to him with his constant smile contradicts him with a gentle, resonant voice: "Einstein was right, but only in your physical system. There are systems in which Einstein's physics no longer applies. How do you imagine we got here? With liquid propellant rocket power?"

As reasonable beings, centuries ahead of Earth technology, the ETs will not intervene in our lives without gentle preparation. Preparation? How?

On October 13, 1917, the aliens demonstrated their presence before 75,000 earthlings in the small Portuguese village of Fatima, disguised as a religious apparition. At the time, they delivered a message addressed to the "highest representative of the Earth" with the request to publish this message in 1960—43 years after the show in the firmament. The message ended up in the Vatican. All popes to the present day have refused to make the content of the so-called "third secret of Fatima" accessible to the public, although the message was actually supposed to come from the (alleged) Mother of God, who is likely to know what she can expect of her highest religious representative on Earth. Subsequently false messages were published and falsehoods produced by Vatican circles. I have scrupulously exposed the whole tissue of lies in my book *The Gods Were Astronauts*.[14] Either way, visitors can still admire the marvelous stained-glass window depicting the so-called "Miracle of the Sun of Fatima" in the magnificent Basilica of Fatima. (See Image 1 of the color insert.)

The popes refuse to make the message of Fatima publicly accessible. Period. Would it not be high time for the extraterrestrials to protest and intervene? Clearly that has not happened, not in 1960 nor later. Why not? Because the ETs know our politics, our religions, our whole social system and, furthermore, do not have the slightest interest in throwing Earth into turmoil. That starts with simple self-interest. A broken planet with millions of angry, disappointed people is of no use to them at all. So they continued to show patience with these fractious beings and gentle preparation for the official contact. The popes, of course, know about this. Since 1960 (at the latest) each one of them knows the truth. Each one of them knows about that contact on October 13, 1917. And each one of them knows that the truth is inexorably approaching. Day for day, year for year. It comes as no surprise to me at all that His Holiness Pope John XXIII (1958–1963), who read the message of Fatima in 1960, died of grief and sorrow. The next pontiff, Pope John Paul V (1963–1978), traveled the world and likely informed all the princes of the different religions about the ETs and the inexorably approaching "Judgment Day of Knowledge." And here it fits the mold perfectly that the next pope, John Paul I, could no longer bear the untruth and went to pieces. Even *before* his election, the future pope had detailed discussions with the nun Lucia—the same Sister Lucia who was the former girl of Fatima. The pope's brother, Edoardo Luciani, reported that after the conversation with Sister Lucia, his brother (the future pope) had been "completely devastated.[15] He exercised his difficult office a mere 33 days. There was subsequently speculation that the pope had been murdered, presumably because he had found out about some corrupt dealings in the Vatican's banking business.[16] And what if things were completely different? After all, the pope knew the truth about Fatima from Sister Lucia. He knew that it had not been the Mother of God who had been revealed there but an extraterrestrial. Did he discuss this fact with high dignitaries? Did he intend to publish it? Was this his death sentence? The fact remains: John Paul I was in office a miserly 33 days. The next pope, John Paul II, exercised his office from 1978 to 2005. He is seen as the Apostle who traveled the world. In each country that he visited he first kissed the ground. A symbolic act? Or did he want to symbolize that this land still belongs to us Earth citizens? Finally, there was Benedict XVI, the first German pope (in office from 2005 to 2013). On February 28, 2013, he retired from his office, which was a unique event in the 1,900-year history of the papacy. The highest Church dignitary, the successor to the Throne of St. Peter, couldn't be bothered anymore. Oh yes, their Holinesses know what is going on. And science?

There is just a very small group that is in the know and it has undertaken not to go public. Why, for God's sake? Why all this stupid secrecy?

Imagine an individual astrophysicist was contacted by an extraterrestrial somehow. What is the man supposed to do now? Call a scientific conference and inform his colleagues?

They would declare him to be insane. And if he could prove his contact? Perhaps through a gift from the ETs that convinces all those present? Now the responsibility of the scientific community kicks in. Every astrophysicist and every astronomer is a highly educated person. Each one of them knows our social system, knows about religion and politics. Each one can imagine the reaction of people. It is clear immediately to each one of the scientists present that humanity is not yet ready for this explosive message. They impose self-censorship on themselves. And this can be proved.

Each year, a SETI conference takes place somewhere in the world under the auspices of the International Academy of Astronautics (the IAA). SETI stands for "Search for Extraterrestrial Intelligence." As long ago as the 1989 SETI conference, the scientists involved decided to introduce self-censorship that would apply to all astronomers and astrophysicists: the "Declaration of Principles Concerning Activities Following the Detection of Extraterrestrial Intelligence."[17] This declaration sets out how scientists must act in the face of an extraterrestrial intelligence.

1. Any individual, public or private research institution, or governmental agency that believes *it has detected* a signal from or *other evidence of extraterrestrial life* (author's italics) should seek to verify that the most plausible explanation for the evidence is the existence of extraterrestrial intelligence...before making any public announcement.

2. *Prior* to making any public announcement that evidence of extraterrestrial intelligence has been

detected, the discoverer should promptly inform all other observers or research organizations that are parties to this declaration.... Parties to this declaration *should not make any public announcement of this information.*

3. Should credible evidence of extraterrestrial intelligence be discovered, an international committee of scientists and other experts should be established.

Understood? Even a scientist, be they ever so high in their profession and, indeed, be able to present concrete evidence for their contact with an ET, may not go public with it. First, everything has to wend its sluggish way through the commissions. There, the decision is taken as to whether people are ready for an extraterrestrial message. But what if a scientist goes off script? Doesn't care one jot about the declaration? They might call a press conference—and that would be end of them. Their own colleagues will stab them in the back. They will have broken the supreme command: Thou shalt not go public. And the media will not take what they say seriously. Just as they do not take seriously the statements of the personalities quoted on pages 31-34.

All nations with the technological capability engage in astronomy. They not only observe the heavens but also search for signals from ETs. Whole forests of parabolic antennas are pointed at the sky. Sensors have been fired into space and robots landed on the surface of Mars. As I am typing these lines, the space probe DAWN is orbiting the planet Ceres in the asteroid belt and is supplying sensational pictures. Pictures, by the way, that also show a mountain with strange white and black stripes and a large rectangle on the ground. It could not be clearer that these are not natural phenomena. Astronomers are desperately seeking a natural explanation for them, but they might equally be traces of mining. At some point, a group of ETs mined raw materials on Ceres. This thought is not allowed to be presented in public—at least not by any serious astronomer. And in general, these are very clever and thoroughly honest people. Should the highly important, astronomical authority of this world be ambushed and told that all its endeavors in the search for extraterrestrial intelligence had been superfluous? The billions spent on parabolic antennas, spacecraft, and robots had been wasted taxpayers' money? Its scientific research down the drain—because the ETs were already here? Here! In the solar system and even on Earth? How should a brilliant astrophysicist like Stephen Hawking, who is looking for extraterrestrial life together with the billionaire Yuri Milner, react? Hawking and Milner started a hundred-million-dollar program in April 2016, to search for life in space. A huge sum spent for no purpose? I can imagine that Stephen Hawking has no wish to know anything about UFOs or any ETs on Earth—until he is contacted personally.

Slowly even skeptics must realize that, not just the public in general, but science as well, must be protected from the appearance of ETs. Science requires censorship as much as the trusting mass of the people. How, then, to proceed despite the evident facts? Claudio Stella, the thorough thinker about contact with ETs, proposes a long preparatory period: "If the adjustment takes place in a distanced, critical, deliberate, and slow way, then there need be less fear of a cultural shock extending as far as the loss of our own cultural orientation and the resulting terrible consequences...."[18]

According to his analysis, it would be wise on the part of the ETs to use a preparatory period in advance of the great event:

> Because such processes can take an irrational course, it may be advisable for the ETs to prepare the earth mentally, culturally, politically, and organizationally for their arrival through direct advance notification. Various forms of advance notice could be used for such a careful, hardly shocking first contact. A technical artifact which can clearly be ascribed to an extraterrestrial civilization might appear, for example, to prepare humankind....[19]

We are in the middle of this preparatory process and very few citizens of the Earth have any inkling of it. Mental and cultural adjustment? For decades the science-fiction films coming out of Hollywood have become ever more sophisticated, technically ever more perfect. Millions of people follow the *Star Wars* series with huge enthusiasm. Since 2009, the History Channel has broadcast the series *Ancient Aliens*. This show focuses on the visits of extraterrestrials over the millennia. Originally there were to be five episodes; there are now 150. *Ancient Aliens* has the highest viewing figures in the history of the History Channel.

A political adjustment? How is this supposed to work on a planet on which religious wars are fought? On which dictators rule their countries and are not interested in any modernization? Every despot, and be he ever so cunning, registers the technical changes in the world. TV programs are broadcast via satellites. Travelers report on their experiences in other countries. The Internet is flourishing everywhere. A country cannot be closed off. Even the most stupid of dictators wants to partake in modern achievements. Since the industry in his own country is incapable of producing a refrigerator or cell phone, he has to acquire technical products from abroad, including arms. The invoices for his imported goods have to be settled with an international currency. His own national currency is of no interest whatsoever to anyone because nothing can be bought with it. The dictator has no alternative other than to fit in with international practices sooner or later. He will be taken into the UN family and has to comply with the relevant agreements. Finally, UN representatives visit his kingdom and citizens from his country travel abroad. If he continues to keep his state isolated, the homemade revolution becomes inevitable. The zeitgeist overcomes every dictatorship.

Most industrialized nations foster democracy and their representatives never tire of recommending this form of government to everyone else. However, a popular democracy as it is practiced in Switzerland, for example, is not feasible internationally. In a democracy the majority wins and the minority acquiesces to this dictate without dispute or, indeed, war. But this requires, before anything else, that all voters are rational. Reading and writing are the minimum requirements, and public education must have progressed to the level that the voting citizens can factually weigh up the pros and cons of a debate. Thanks to the media, the masses can be easily influenced. Does that mean clearing the way for the oligarchs? For the owners of these magical channels? Democracies have inbuilt rules to contain the power of the super-rich. These rules work, more or less.

What would happen if an ET allied themselves with a rich family and persuaded these super capitalists to publicize an embassy of the extraterrestrials through the media controlled by the rich family? There might even be an arrangement. The rich person is given some unique technical know-how by the ET, which he could patent and manufacture in his industries, making the family even richer. And what is the benefit for the ET?

They have broken the rules that their species agreed with another group. Other rich people—or also the military or states!—could attack the exposed oligarch, scorn his product, call him internationally to order. His freedom to travel and that of his staff could be restricted, his accounts frozen, and so on. The super-rich family would also have to fit in. It, more than others, knows the international conventions, and it too wants to be a respected member of human society. The ET would have no benefit from going it alone. Intergalactic rules might even apply in the universe, something like a "Milky Way UN," which prohibits individual ETs from taking up contact with individuals on another planet. Perhaps the ET would risk being excluded from their community. They could be isolated and cut off from their technical bases.

If everything is so complicated, with whom are the extraterrestrials supposed to establish contact? Apparently their technological superiority may not be used—a destroyed planet is of no use to them and they can find raw materials for free in the solar system. An agreement may not be concluded with just a single nation because the nation concerned would immediately have an advantage over the others. Single persons may not be given an advantage and, even if such a person received exclusive and valuable information, they would not be taken seriously by public opinion. With whom, for all the world, are the ETs supposed to communicate? Who is left?

Intelligent people who have the competence to convene a body committed to silence. Thanks to its awareness of its responsibility, such a group would be suitable for judging the consequences of a contact. Precisely, this variant is currently happening.

The ETs are supposed to prepare humanity "mentally, culturally, politically and organizationally"[20] for their visit? But they have to start somewhere. This has been happening since Fatima in 1917. For decades they have shown themselves intermittently. The earthlings called it UFOs. Reasonable people shrugged their shoulders and at best laughed about it. But the number of occasions grew. Stupid and clever books about UFOs were published, and intellectual giants and simple workers were among the people affected. The UFO literature grew into millions. Then there were encounters of the third and fourth kind—ETs conversed with humans and even invited them into their spaceships. There are authenticated reports about that.[21] This was followed by the kidnapping of individual people. Down-to-earth scientists cried indignantly, "Stop this nonsense!" "Intolerable!" But the nonsense only lasted until it was scientifically verified because the ETs had given some of their victims implants. They could be surgically removed and physically and chemically analyzed.[22, 23, 24] There was scientific verification at least for those who were seriously interested in knowing. Year after year, ever bigger international UFO conferences were convened, attended by thousands including an increasing number of scientists. For decades, I tended to see myself as an opponent of the UFO community. Too much nonsense was being peddled. Then, after meeting some wonderful people, including some extraordinary personalities, I gradually had to revise my opinion. That is what I wrote in the first chapter of my last book about five UFO cases that definitively cannot be proved wrong. I knew all the eye-witnesses personally.[25] And when someone has delved so deeply into the subject, has taken the opposing arguments of the skeptics into account, then someone like me can no longer keep silent. We are called upon to show the courage of our convictions.

But how, in what form, did the first extraterrestrials contact individual scientists? Did they appear to them like angels in a dream? Storm into their bedrooms at night like goblins? Did they disguise themselves as speaking dogs or clever parrots?

After the ETs had quietly and secretly kidnapped individual earthlings, samples of sperm and ovum were taken from them.[26] Human extraterrestrials were created. That is the people about whom Canada's ex-defense minister said, "Some of the extraterrestrials look like us and could walk down the street without anyone noticing."[27] The comprehensive knowledge of these "ambassadors" impressed every scientist who had been contacted to such an extent that they—to use a colloquial expression—could have been knocked over with a feather. These brilliant people who were taken into the confidence of the aliens are aware of their responsibility toward humanity. Inevitably secret groups formed; that is how it works in human society. And of course the group of people contacted wanted something in return from the ETs. We simply cannot change our spots; the group accordingly tried to negotiate. That might have gone something like this: We accept your presence, and we will protect your anonymity until the majority of people can digest the existence of extraterrestrials without panicking. How about, in return, showing us some tiny aspect of your phenomenal technology? In a next step it is contractually agreed that the acquired knowledge may only be used for the benefit of humanity as a whole—an agreement that both parties must comply with. Earth people are aware of the terrible reaction of their fellow humans if the ETs were to appear over sold-out football stadiums. The extraterrestrials equally so and, furthermore, a destroyed planet and freaked-out humanity would be of no use to them. In the worst case of a breach of the agreement, the extraterrestrials could still use the threat of their arms. So within a short period of time, an earthly UFO has been built in a super-secret facility, which could just as well fly to the stars as its extraterrestrial model. How did Dr. Benjamin Robert Rich, the director of the Lockheed Skunk Works, in which the stealth bomber was developed, put it? "We already have the possibility of flying to the stars.... Whatever you can imagine, we know how it works. We have the technology to bring ET home. No, it will not require a lifetime to do it. We know how it works. We could have the opportunity to fly to the stars."[28] The U.S. astronaut Edgar Mitchell is of the same opinion: "Not all UFOs are in fact extraterrestrial in origin. Some of them are our own development...but we are by no means at the technological level of those who visit us."[29]

Why does every American government class dramatic UFO sightings, unmistakable over-flights of its own territory reported by pilots, as harmless? Is it simply what the skeptics claim? That no one, neither a U.S. defense secretary nor any reasonable scientist takes the subject seriously? UFOs and everything associated with them are baloney, total nonsense, a figment of the imagination? And the people with their objective warnings are misled and should not be taken seriously? Sorry! The problem is the reverse. The skeptics and the "reasonable people" who want to stand with both feet on the ground are uninformed. They do not *know* what is going on. Every person, without exception, whom I quoted at the beginning of this chapter, was originally a skeptic. None of them considered UFOs to be an extraterrestrial reality before then. All of them stood on the ground of alleged reason until they were initiated. And it requires effort to get to this information—it does not just drop into a person's lap. After all, we are still dealing with well-guarded secrets intended to prevent humanity from going mad. Meanwhile, however, UFOs have been recorded by all military systems. There is a wealth of outstanding radar and visual data, clear statements from fighter pilots and air force generals internationally. And none of these witnesses are a sandwich short of a picnic; none of them are crackpots. None of them are irresponsible. Yet the U.S. government does not see the slightest danger to national security?[30] When, however, a foreign aircraft, which could be shot down immediately, crosses the U.S. border, national security is invoked without ado. There could not be a clearer indication of the existence of a secret agreement than the downright absurdly indifferent behavior of the U.S. authorities with regard to UFOs. Woe betide any Russian aircraft or foreign submarine violating American sovereign territory. All hell immediately breaks loose, including in the media. Yet UFOs do not exist even though hundreds of them have been documented and nailed down both electronically and visually.

Because the right hand does not know what the left hand is doing, the authorities tie themselves up in exquisite knots. The announcement is made that UFOs do not exist, yet the U.S. Department of Transportation published a memo for pilots on February 9, 2012, titled "Section 8. Unidentified Flying Objects (UFO) Reports." It tells pilots where they should report UFO sightings, specifically to "Bigelow Aerospace Advanced Space Studies (BAASS)" and provides a telephone number and email address.

Long before that, the Ministry of Defense (MoD) informed its staff of the following on June 24, 1965: "Our policy is to downplay the subject of UFOs and to avoid attaching undue attention or publicity to it."[31]

As long ago as 1953, when UFO sightings were slowly coming into fashion, the CIA, the U.S. secret service, issued the following guidelines in the Robertson Panel Report:

> All authorities in the secret service network are encouraged to influence the mass media for the purpose of debunking and infiltrate civilian UFO research groups...UFO reports should be made implausible and ridiculous...public interest in UFO events should be expressly undermined...and secret service agents should ensure that the facts are withheld from leading researchers through targeted disinformation."[32]

There is no other word for this than "conspiracy." By the authorities. Period. And the present shows how the instructions of the CIA were followed and carried out worldwide. Anyone who wants to be taken seriously thinks UFOs are nonsense.

Presumably, the ETs would prefer to negotiate with a world government that is responsible for the whole of humanity. But such a body does not exist on Earth. (Although some groups are working hard to achieve it.) That leaves the UN. In this case, the discussion would have to be with UN delegates and at some point the UN General Assembly would have to be involved. That, presumably, is the long-term goal. At the present time, however, pure suicide. ETs before the UN and the eggs would be broken. Total panic.

The ETs could simply ignore our concerns and interfere when and where they wanted. They could impose their legal order on us and totally disregard parliaments and the UN. That would be dictatorship with the consequences already discussed. The same applies to a kind of protectorate. Claudio Stella considers it feasible that the Earth could become the protectorate of an intergalactic community.[33] That would be impossible without the political will of the Earth community (UN); it would ultimately be no different to an ET dictatorship. But now the aliens *want* something from us (I will get to that). The Earth, or we human beings, must possess something that is of interest to the others. With a dictatorship out of the running, that only leaves negotiation. But negotiations do not work anywhere in the universe without a legal basis. The aliens know their law and we know ours, as do countries all around the world. They all have laws of their own, but there is also the superior law of the world community. A consensus will have to be found. Ultimately, it will come down to human beings expecting a lot more from the aliens than the ETs expect from us.

How does communication faster than the speed of light work? How about interstellar space travel without our primitive liquid fuel rockets? How have you come to grips in your development with environmental problems? Energy problems? How did the different races actually arise? How many species are there out there? What was there before the Big Bang? What is God? How can we extremely extend our life? Are there also criminals in your world? How do you deal with them? Do you use transportation to move about? How does it work? And your social system? Capitalism? Communism? Socialism? Democracy? Dictatorship? Monarchy? What policies meet the requirements of all classes? Is there something like a "galactic club"? How does one become a member? What rules have to be complied with? What kind of clothing do you wear? How is it made? What kind of metal or other alloys do you have? Where are they used? Are there wars in the universe? Why? Who against whom?

Our curiosity is unending. At some point, we will be faced with the choice of being galactically involved or subsisting as an underdeveloped planet, cut off from the rest of the Milky Way, possibly to self-destruction and a new start.

Just think: A presence of the ETs visible to all citizens of Earth robs many global players of their power. Religions, cardinals, popes, mullahs, chief rabbis, and so on belong just as much to the losers as national governments. "Politicians must come to grips with the question of losing their power from one day to the next if they have to hand over their power to a world organization.... The elites will lose their pre-rogatives," writes Claudio Stella.[34]

Why? Won't people simply adapt? If only. And irrespec-tive of the leading political and financial groups, there are myriads of religious communities on Earth. The so-called "prophets," the self-styled "Apostles" of Jesus, the "elect," the saints, and, not to mention, the hypocrites, will never admit that they have for decades led their believers in a merry dance. The lay person has no idea how many churches there are in total and that each one of them claims to be the only true one. The following incomplete list of existing religious communities should give us food for thought:

- Church of Constantinople (Ecumenical Patriarchate of Constantinople).

- Orthodox Autocephalous Church of Albania (Archdiocese of Albania).

- Orthodox Autocephalous Church of Alexandria and All Africa (Patriarchate of Alexandria).

- Church of America (Archdiocese of America).

- Church of Bulgaria (Patriarchate von Bulgaria; Bulgarian Orthodox Church).

- Autocephalous Church of All Georgia (Patriarchate of Georgia; Georgian Apostolic Orthodox Church).

- Autocephalous Orthodox Church of All Greece (Archdiocese of Greece; Greek Orthodox Church).

- Autocephalous Orthodox Church of Jerusalem and All Palestine (Patriarchate of Jerusalem).

- Autocephalous Orthodox Church of All Poland (Archdiocese of Poland; Polish Orthodox Church).

- Autocephalous Orthodox Church of Antioch and All the East (Patriarchate von Antioch; Rum Orthodox Church).

- Church of Romania (Patriarchate of Romania; Romanian Orthodox Church).

- Church of Moscow and All Russia (Patriarchate of Moscow und All Russia; Russian Orthodox Church).

- Church of Cyprus (Archdiocese of Cyprus; Cypriot Orthodox Church).

- Macedonian Orthodox Church.

- Orthodox Church of Bessarabia.

- Montenegrin Orthodox Church.

- Ukrainian Autocephalous Orthodox Church.

- Turkish Orthodox Patriarchate.

- French Orthodox Church.

- Abkhazian Orthodox Church.

- Croatian Orthodox Church.

- Moldovan Orthodox Church.

- Belarusian Orthodox Church.

- Pomorian Old Orthodox Church.

- Orthodox Old Rite Church.

- Russian Orthodox Old Rite Church.

- Russian Old Orthodox Church.

- Coptic Orthodox Church (Egypt).

- British Orthodox Church: This church, founded by Raymond Ferrete in 1866, calls upon the tradition of the Celtic Church existing until the Synod of Cashel of 1172.

- Roman Catholic Church (also Catholic Church).

- Philippine Independent Church or Aglipayan Church after its founder Gregorio Aglipay, independent of the Roman Catholic Church since 1902.

- Holy Cross Old Catholic Diocese of Minnesota (Bishop James Judd).

- Old Catholic Diocese of Napa, until 2010 Old Catholic Church in California (Bishop Robert Fuentes).

- Old Catholic Diocese of New England (Bishop Rosemary Ananis).

- Old Catholic Diocese of Washington, D.C. (Bishop Robert Fuentes).

- American Old Catholic Church in Colorado (Bishop Dan Gincig).

- Apostolic Catholic Church in Florida (Bishop Chuck Leigh).

- Ecumenical Catholic Church in New York (Bishop Peter Brennan).

- Old Catholic Church in Louisiana (Bishop Allen Jimenez).

Other independent Old Catholic churches that belong to the World Council of Churches through the International Council of Community Churches (ICCC) are:

- American Catholic Church in California (Bishop Lou Bordisso).

- Apostolic Catholic Church in Washington (Bishop David Strong).

- Ecumenical Catholic Church in Connecticut (Bishop Lorraine Bouffard).

- Open Episcopal Church in Great Britain (Bishop Jonathan Blake).

- Biserica Catolica Independenta in Romania.

- The Society of Saint Pius X and other traditionalist or sedevacantist groups.

- Swiss Reformed Church.

- Evangelical Church of Egypt (Synod of the Nile).

- Evangelical Presbyterian Church, Ghana.

- Assyrian Evangelical Church.

- Presbyterian Church in Ireland.

- Presbyterian Church in Cameroon.

- Presbyterian Church of Nigeria.

- Church of Scotland.

- Free Church of Scotland.

- United Free Church of Scotland.

- Cumberland Presbyterian Church.

- Presbyterian Church (the largest Presbyterian church in the USA).

- Working Group of Mennonite Brethren Communities.

- Federation of Anabaptist Communities.

- Mennonite Free Church of Austria.

- Union of Evangelical Free Church Congregations.

- Union of Baptist Congregations in Austria.

- Union of Swiss Baptist Congregations.
- American Baptist Churches USA.
- Southern Baptist Convention.
- Congregation for Christ.
- Moravian Church.
- African Methodist Episcopal Church.
- Church of the Nazarene.
- Evangelical Church of Czech Brethren.
- United Church of Christ.
- Christian Church (Disciples of Christ).
- Seventh-day Adventist Church.
- Assemblies of God.
- Federation of Pentecostal Churches.
- Church of God.
- Ecclesia Congregation of Christians.
- Mülheim Association of Free Churches and Evangelical Communities (oldest German Pentecostal association).
- Word of Faith.
- Swiss Pentecostal Mission.
- International Christian Fellowship.
- Jesus Freaks.

- Schwenkfelder Church (six congregations in Pennsylvania).

- Shakers (are deemed to be the smallest existing Christian confession).

- Universalists.

- Apostolic Church of Queensland.

- Apostolic Church of South-Africa—Apostle Unity.

- Federation of Reformed Apostolic Communities.

- Apostle Ministry of Jesus Christ.

- Wiesbaden Apostolic Community.

- Federation of Apostolic Communities.

- Het Apostolisch Genootschap.

- Christian Science.

- Church of God (Seventh Day).

- Unification Church.

- Jehovah's Witnesses.

- Adamites.

- Arianism.

- Fifth Monarchy Men.

- Gallicanism.

- Bohemian Brethren.

- Hussites.

- Huguenots.

- Congregationalists.

- Brethren of the Free Spirit.

- Pataria.

- Paulicianism.

- Puritans.

- Ranters.

- Socinianism.

- Zionites.

- Mormons.

- Scientologists.

- The Church of the Rosicrucians.

That was just a little more than a hundred Christian churches. Then there is the world community of Muslims with its respective subdivisions: Shi'ites, Sunnis, Wahhabites, Salafists, and so on. And each religious community is firmly convinced that it possesses the one "true" religion—the single, immutable truth, very often directly inspired by God or at least a Holy Spirit. For these people, it is simply incomprehensible that their faith is suddenly no longer correct.

Millions of high priests, sect leaders, the "blessed," the "illuminated," or otherwise-inspired people would never be able to cope with the new facts. All of them will admonish their followers not to listen to the extraterrestrials under any circumstances, curse them, and fight them "in the name of God."

For how much longer will the ETs watch earthly egoism before they act? When will they have had enough? When will their patience be exhausted, the limits of their empathy be reached? Have they set a deadline for their scientific contact persons on Earth? For so long we will leave you in peace, but there will come a time when enough is enough? And then? Will they simply disappear without a trace for the next few thousand years or will there be the complete divine shock for humanity? Which values are more important for the ETs?

In the past, and I know quite a lot about this, the extraterrestrials never revealed themselves to huge crowds of people. They always showed themselves to biblical figures such as Moses and his brother Aaron, the Patriarch Abraham, wise Solomon, or the Prophet Ezekiel in small groups, at least according to what "Holy Scripture" says. They did indeed subsequently take Enoch, later misunderstood as a "prophet," into their spaceship and instructed him in language and science, but they did not cause a shock to any crowds. On the other hand, they struck mercilessly, rampaged terribly if an experiment went wrong. Cities such as Sodom and Gomorrah were destroyed with the same brutality as, ultimately, the whole of humanity through a deliberately caused flood. Deliberate? The Flood was not a natural event?

Stories of the Flood are a universal fact in religions and myths. Be it the Bible, the Sumerian Gilgamesh epic, the "Epic of Creation," the "Enuma Elish" of the Babylonians, the Book of Mormon, the Kogi in Columbia, the Hopi in Arizona, the Maya in Central America, or the Dogon in Africa, a "God" always warns human beings of the Flood. All of them knew of the coming deluge far in advance. And not just only two weeks in advance like today's weather forcast. The moment in time was set long before, the countdown has started. Without exception, all adherents were instructed to build a specific, watertight ship. Logically, none of the gods acted "omnipotently," none gave human beings a boat as a gift. None of the "heavenly beings" who had come down to Earth possessed the omnipotence to produce a ship just like that in the blink of an eye or by snapping their fingers. Every ship that was built required technology. Shipbuilding *is* technology. And each of the pseudo gods described the coming Flood as a punishment. The human spawn of the time was *meant* to be destroyed. Clearly a genetic program had gone wrong. That, at least, is what many traditions say. According to the Book of Enoch, Chapter 106-13, "A great destruction will come over the whole earth, a deluge...great punishment will come over the earth and the earth will be cleaned of all dirt.... That is why I will bring a deluge to the earth..."[35]

What decision will the ETs take today? In the past, they left us unmistakable signs, enticed us to follow the trail. These signs *do* exist; those who want to *have* recognized them.[36, 37, 38] Created thousands of years ago, they are nevertheless addressed to a technologically and scientifically oriented society of the future which *had* to stumble across them. Millions of enlightened Earth inhabitants have meanwhile understood this. And, as planned, the message from the past has promptly added up. But science, whose real task should actually be to further knowledge, indignantly turns its back. Nothing to do with me! It does not want to acknowledge that it was deliberately led astray. And afterward it is difficult to admit to having been used as a "useful idiot." In psychology, it is called repression. And the media, always concerned for its alleged integrity, is not allowed to report objectively about something that millions of people are concerned with. We have created a two-class society. A small group of people in the know is opposed by a mighty majority of those who don't know and do not want to know in their lovely idyllic world. But for how much longer?

Does every intelligent species out there actually have to engage in space travel? Do they *have* to do it because it is dictated by their insatiable curiosity? Because they need raw materials? Because their home planet, their home sun is exploding, burning up? Because their galaxy is being swallowed up by a black hole? Or is colliding with another galaxy? That is also relevant for us. According to NASA calculations, the so-called "Smith's Cloud" will collide with our Milky Way in 30 million years. There will be gigantic fireworks of destroyed celestial bodies, and two million new stars will be created. The Smith's Cloud consists primarily of hydrogen gas, currently still about 8,000 light years distant from the Earth. But it is approaching us at a speed of 240 kilometers per second. If our astronomers are able to calculate what will happen in 30 million years, then extraterrestrial astrophysicists can do the same. They, too, will know how long before they crash and will seek out new habitats before then. Space travel is a *must* for every society. Others think differently.

In a lengthier article in the specialist journal *IBIS,* astronomer William Hoesek argues that ETs wouldn't engage in space travel.[39] How so? Hoesek argues that the raw materials on every planet will run out at some point. But people are made such that they do not plan for the long term—meaning for centuries and longer. Be it the state or private companies, neither invests with centuries in mind because they need short-term results for their shareholders or voters. If humans were to send a spaceship on the search for raw materials, the people left at home would have no idea whether the crew of the spaceship had been successful or would return empty-handed. And no human society would spend perhaps a billion dollars on such an uncertain venture. People live for the short term and want to see quick results. Furthermore, the construction of a gigantic generational spaceship would not only swallow up vast amounts of money but also raw materials—precisely those materials that are becoming scarce on the home planet. Logically, such valuable raw materials could not be squandered on an immensely expensive space adventure, the results of which—if any—would not become apparent for centuries. The same "earthly" logic also applies, William Hoesek says, to extrasolar civilizations. The results of his analysis are correspondingly sobering:

1. In order to obtain help from another civilization, we would have to know "the others" and at least be in radio contact with them.

2. The civilization on that distant planet would have to be more technically advanced than us.

3. That civilization would have to be in a position to receive and understand our messages.

4. It would have to make available the raw materials we seek.

5. It would have to be willing to share its technology and raw materials with us.

6. We would have to be capable of understanding its tools and instructions.

7. The ETs out there would also know that their raw materials would be exhausted at some point. Hence they would be unlikely to give raw materials to other civilizations.[40]

That might all make sense from an economic perspective; it is, nevertheless, incorrect. After all, no gigantic spaceship is needed to seek and mine raw materials in space. We never have to go to far distant locations. We have masses of raw materials in the asteroid belt between Mars and Jupiter. Distant suns, too, are orbited by more than one planet and meteorites fly through all of space. Neither are generational spaceships required to discover the geological composition of distant planets. Thanks to spectral analysis, we can already do that with our super telescopes. Furthermore, innumerable probes can be sent out that radio back their findings to the home planet. Then, earthly lifespans should never be transposed to alien civilizations. The space-traveling ETs will know ways to extend life. Finally, space travel at interstellar distances will not be undertaken with our outdated liquid propellant rockets in any case. Quite different possibilities will exist in the future—and thus different times. Dr. Hoesek's views are based on false assumptions.

The ETs have left traces in the past. Lots of them. They are described in ancient sacred writings as well as in the landscape. The completely straight lines that have been inscribed across the earth for thousands of years were not created by our Stone Age forebears because they had nothing better to do, but they followed orders from the ETs only to establish their sacred sites in specific locations.[41] The stone circles of Stonehenge do not happen to indicate the distances between the planets of our solar system. Their astronomical teachers were those "gods." Similarly, the columns of menhirs in Brittany, France, which always reveal the same distances or precisely half thereof, and which are full of Pythagorean triangles, are not inspired by any whim of nature. Our Stone Age blokes received their geometrical orders directly from the ETs. Long before Pythagoras.

And today? We human beings should be prepared for a peaceful arrival of the extraterrestrials. Where are the signs, other than Fatima, the UFOs, films, books, and TV series? They lie in the open landscape, yet our blind intellectual world, including the "rational" media, has long since managed to ridicule these signs, to discredit everything.

Crop circles? Every Tom, Dick, and Harry knows about the fakes! After all, the thoroughly earthly artists are revealed in magazines and on television. Clearly recognizable, they demonstrate their skill in creating magnificent pictures in the landscape. What else is there to be said about it? Why waste time and money to confirm simple fakes?

The whole weird business started in Australia in the area surrounding Tully in Queensland. In the autumn of 1966, farmer George Pedley discovered six circles in a corn field. They were classed as the product of small tornadoes. Others described them as a "UFO nest." Then the phenomenon began to spread like a virus to other countries: Canada, Italy, Mexico, the United States, and, of course, the country where there has always been weird events, England. Reasonable and unreasonable theories were advanced. They were the tracks of tornadoes, of rutting pigs or other animals. Ants or termites were responsible for the circles and, in general, they were damage from hail. Next on the list were unknown force fields active below the surface of the earth. I read somewhere that certain animals would run in circles when in heat, and I also read about the assumption that the riddle could be explained quite reasonably through mushrooms. Then it was the turn of hot air balloons, which had gone down in impossible locations, and of course we must not forget the footpads of UFOs. The next theory took recourse to solar wind as a solution or lightning strikes with an electrical discharge to subterranean water courses. Moles or a collection of worms were made responsible, and high frequency signals were supposedly at fault for the symbols in the fields. The physicist Dr. Terence Maeden (University of Oxford and Dalhousie University Halifax, Canada) connected these impossible events with "atmospheric physics," "plasma vortices," and "electromagnetic fields."[42]

None of this was sufficient for profound thinkers because every explanation had convincing counter arguments. Did the world-famous psychologist C.G. Jung not write about strange lights and celestial phenomena that would appear as the messengers of great, collective changes in thinking?[43] Even about "psychic forces" and "events which would be incomprehensible to people?" Could it therefore be that these symbols "might have their origin in the imagination of individuals or the imagination fed by collective dreams and visions?"[44] Or did the community of human beings not generate a "collective, cultural impulse which released sufficient energy to cause a wave of unusual events?"[45]

Over the years, all explanations, be they ever so reasonable and factual, faded away because the drawings on the ground simply refused to cooperate. If originally the pictures appeared in grain fields, they now suddenly grew in fields of barley, rapeseed, and even maize. If in the beginning they were simple circles, increasing numbers of ellipses and wonderful, partially interlaced works of art began to be created. The pictures are their own proof. None of this fit any longer with ants, termites, mushrooms, worms, tornadoes, rutting beasts, lightning strikes, or plasma vortices. The pictures displayed intelligence, so fakers had to come to the rescue! Some wise guys were making fools of all of us and having a good laugh about the human ability to make things up. The first to "out" themselves were the British pensioners "Doug and

Dave." In front of the camera, they stated that they had faked all the crop circles to make the subject ridiculous. Their revelations soon turned out to be a huge bluff. Several mighty shapes appeared in various places where the busy pensioners could never have been. That included the picture of August 8, 2008, in Milk Hill, Wiltshire. It consists of 44 circles of various sizes, interlaced at the center with various additional representations. Or the geometrical shape of the "hypercube," created on July 17, 2010, in Fosbury Camp, Wiltshire. Here, there is not a single circle, but only symmetrical lines forming a massive hexagon with a cube in the center. When the busy pensioners Doug and Dave could not be held liable, other fakers had to do.

At some point (I can no longer remember when), a young man announced on a German television program that he and his group had faked all the symbols. Cockily he drew attention to one detail that people had to be aware of: All the circles, lines, and so on always bordered on a tractor track or beaten path. A pure lie. Hundreds of circles and lines are not connected at any point with a track, however insignificant it might be. A picture like the so-called "magnetic field formation" not far from the Avebury stone circle is so complex that not even a company of soldiers could have faked it overnight.

On March 4, 2015, a complex formation appeared in a maize field near Icara, Santa Marta (Brazil); on January 4 of the same year, a group of interlinking circles appeared near Guadalajara, Mexico, also in a maize field. On May 8, 2015, there were formations in Fangshan district near Beijing,

China. From June to September of the same year, there were further extraordinary formations in various locations in Italy.[46] Even Germany, skeptical about crop circles, marveled on July 16, 2015, about a shape in a grain field. It was near Fürstenfeldbruck in Bavaria. And, hard as it is to believe, a picture near Fürstenfeldbruck was even printed in the major German magazines *Focus* and *Spiegel*—without a mocking commentary!

Meanwhile, the riddle of the crop circles has spread to about 50 countries. Sophisticated teams of fakers must be at work worldwide. The logical conclusion—or are we being deliberately misled, as with the UFOs? The editors of the 150-part History Channel TV series *Ancient Aliens* wanted to find out. They sent their clever commentator Giorgio Tsoukalos to England. He was to commission two well-known fakers to make a copy of an already existing crop circle. So "Russel and John," as the two were called, stuck their poles into the ground, laid out trails, fixed ropes, and seized their "stalk stompers." (That is what the small boards are called which are used to flatten the grain.) The boards have a rope attached to both ends. This rope is put over the shoulder and then the board is pressed down on the grain and lifted again by the rope for the next step.

In fact, Russel and John managed to produce quite a reasonable copy of the original within 210 minutes. Drones flew over both pictures. Only a few differences could be discerned from the air. But what did a closer inspection reveal?

In the meantime, a team from the University of Michigan had started to investigate the phenomenon scientifically. The physicist Dr. Eltjo Haselhoff demonstrated the differences between "real" and "fake" in front of the camera. The typical signs of a real crop circle are the following: the blossoms are not damaged or broken, in contrast to the fake made with the "stalk stomper." The same applies to the way the stalks are bent. With the "stomping method" they are broken or at least lacerated. Not so with the mysterious shapes that did not involve any human activity. Curiously, all so-called "apical nodes" display an extension of 172 percent in comparison to the compressed stalks in the fake circles. The second and third node on the stalk has veritably burst from the inside. This points to a short discharge of energy that must have occurred in the stalk. Dr. Haselhoff demonstrated it in front of the camera: Various stalks were taken from the crop circle and put under the microscope. The stalks in the middle showed longer, burst nodes than those on the periphery of the circle. "The differences are like between a horse and an elephant," the physicist explained.[47] The burst nodes are longest in the center and grow smaller toward the outside. The stalks can be shown to have burst because of electromagnetic energy. It is the trigger of the phenomenon.[48] Giorgio Tsoukalos, the commentator of the TV program, said, "I find it strange and discouraging that a phenomenon like the crop circles is not being investigated in depth by science. The circles are dismissed from the beginning as fakes although there is undeniable evidence that they are genuine."

He is right. As long ago as 1990, a Centre for Crop Circle Studies was set up in England—where else?—to investigate the riddle in a squeaky clean scientific way. In the foreword to the book *The Crop Circle Enigma*, the archaeologist Michael Green wrote, "Meanwhile the phenomena are revealed to us in astonishing diversity, in mighty proportions and in downright awe-inspiring beauty.... Various strange circumstances accompany the appearance of the circles. They include, above all, high frequency signals which appear to be subject to specific laws."[49] And Professor Archie Roy, honorary member of the School of Physics and Astronomy of the University of Glasgow and a number of other recognized astronomical institutes, speaks of an "immense riddle" facing physics. The old gentleman knows his history of science. He says, "The whole history of scientific discovery consists of the outsider being declared to be mad by the so-called specialist world—in order finally to triumph after all the contempt and be elected a genius."[50]

The TV program *Ancient Aliens* also showed irrefutable film clips that are quite shocking. The observer sees white circles or spheres floating in the air above a field, including over a track, and a tractor driving along. Within seconds, an amazing picture is created under the shining spheres. As if on command, the stalks lie flat and form into a wonderful and complex work of art. The British Centre for Crop Circle Studies has meanwhile published such films and lets the evidence speak for itself.[51] Thus, 145 of such circles were created within 16 minutes near the Stone Age complex of Stonehenge. And recently, perfect microscopic balls made of a melted material have been discovered in these curious formations. The first were found by accident at Martinson Farm in Midala (Saskatchewan), Canada, after the earth had been sifted there. Meanwhile, they have also been captured in sieves at other locations.

Ralph Noyes, an ex-civil servant in the British air ministry, who later became an under-secretary of state, noted a *development* in the riddle of these pictures: It is no longer correct to refer to crop circles.[52] The depictions are growing in size, diversity, and complexity. If in the 1970s and 1980s they were still circles with a diameter of 10 to 20 meters, today's formations extend for hundreds of meters and often consist of more than a hundred individual parts, which combine into an awesomely beautiful "pictogram." (See Images 2–10 in the color insert.) Fakers, and be they ever so sophisticated, can no longer keep up. Neither could a company of soldiers of the British Army. Sites at which pictures appeared in previous years are kept under observation with automatic cameras. Groups of volunteers support the nightly checks. The wise guys are out of the picture, even if there is still the occasional stray one. On the other hand, researchers with a scientific background are growing increasingly baffled and are searching for a common factor. John Mitchell says, "The impression is growing that there is a specific reference to something."[53] But what? What is the intention of the "circle builders"? The Master of Science and former astronomer at the Royal Greenwich Observatory, George Wingfield, asserts that we are dealing with some kind of *non-human intelligence.* "The messages speak of an extension of human consciousness."[54] The archaeologist Michael Green said, "I am convinced that the source is intelligent in nature and that they are gradually revealing their ideas in accordance with a plan."[55] Meanwhile, Terry Wilson from England has published a remarkable story about the crop circles. The phenomenon is documented worldwide with precise dates and locations, and it is also shown that strange formations were already documented in the 16th and 17th centuries.[56]

Who is this intelligence supposed to be? Does this "unknown" power have no other possibility than to make itself noticed through "pictures in the fields"? Why not direct communication through our media? Why no awesomely beautiful pictures in the night sky? Or interference on our television screens that gradually reveals itself as a pictogram? Counter question: Why don't UFOs show themselves over a sold-out football stadium even though that would be technically possible?

I assume all these things would be possible but "the others" want it like this right now. People are intended to marvel and talk, write and marvel. Slowly we are to be made aware of the other dimension without ambush, without violence, and without dictatorship, yet visible for everyone. Whereby other researchers (including myself) have noticed that many of the grandiose formations are emerging out of the ground near Stone Age complexes, such as Stonehenge, Avebury Ring, Silbury Hill, or the "White Horse" at Uffington, all of them in England. (I heard that the same is true of pictograms in Australia and Mexico. And in the United States, the pictures are created near Indian burial mounds.) How is the past connected with this?

Our early history is more mysterious than how we learned it in school. There we were told that our ancestors, only just descended from the apes, had vegetated in caves, groomed the lice out of their fur, occasionally hunted a mammoth or other animal, and in general chewed on berries and roots. May well be. But another group of Stone Age families behaved in a highly intellectual way. Their astronomical and geometrical achievements prove it. Furthermore, our diligent archaeologists are moving the Stone Age architectural marvels ever further into the past. Current dating is no longer correct.

Around 18,400 years ago, the Mediterranean sea level lay 35 meters lower than it is today. This is shown by a cave system with painted walls that lies 35 meters below the water. It is situated at Cap Morgiou (east of Marseille, France). Ruins have meanwhile been found under water in all the world's oceans.[57] The sea level has risen worldwide. If we thought that the first building phase of the stone circle of Stonehenge occurred in 2,800 BC, the complex is meanwhile (at least) 2,000 years older. The Great Pyramid in Egypt is the first planned high-rise building in antiquity, it used to be said, built in 2,500 BC. Yet the circular complex of Göbekli Tepe in Turkey is 8,000 years older.[58] The approximately 400 rock paintings in the Chauvet Cave (near Vallon-Pont-d'Arc, France) were dated to about 20,000 BC after their discovery. The latest C14 analyses produce a definitive age of 37,000 years. And even in Germany, which, due to its recent history wants to avoid anything to do with nationalism, ever more prehistoric riddles are appearing that are all somehow connected with the starry sky. About 7,000 years ago, there existed in what is today Lower Bavaria several circular complexes with a diameter of between 50 and 180 meters. Without exception, they have an astronomical orientation and frequently several of these stone or wood circles are lined up like pearls on a string. The same applies to Lower Austria, Poland, and Hungary.[59, 60] The circular palisade of Goseck in Saxony-Anhalt, Germany, has a circumference of 75 meters, and like all the others, it is a so-called "sun temple." That is, astronomical, and its age is at least 5,000 BC.[61] Near Künzing in Bavaria, the "Stone Age blokes" jammed 2,000 oak tree trunks into the ground. The same applies to innumerable dolmens and menhirs.

Astronomy played a central role in the heads of the "stoneagers." And we modern people only have super-clever answers as to the *why*. They were "light-pointer instruments," "playing fields," and "secret locations for male rituals," up to and including the most naïve of all answers: they had been calendars.[62] The Stone Age complexes show the intelligence of their planners. These clever architects will also have noticed in nature when the first insects appeared, when the buds opened, or the fruits ripened in the autumn. A small scratch on their cave wall was sufficient to register when the sun rose increasingly earlier or later. A wooden stick in the ground was sufficient to determine when the shadows were longest and shortest. Determining the equinox did not need a gigantic calendar complex. Dragging monoliths weighing several tons about and grinding them down to build a calendar was as necessary as a hole in the head. Furthermore, the command from the high priest, "Spring has come, the seed needs to be sown" would have been no use whatsoever if winter in the relevant year lasted longer than normal and there was another snowfall in the middle of April. It is time to think of something smarter than different versions of a calendar.

Our ancestors followed their celestial cult for one reason alone: because of the gods. It was the gods who had descended from the heavens, their lights moved in the night sky, and their disciples had instructed human beings in various fields of knowledge. Our Stone Age artists were *meant* to build astronomically aligned buildings. Their descendants—us!—should take notice, become puzzled, and seek causes. That is precisely what is happening now. We have *no alternative* because the creature in our heads causing us disquiet has a name: curiosity. No intelligence in the universe can do anything about curiosity—otherwise it would not be intelligence. So who are these beings racing about in UFOs who have caused magnificent art works to be created in the landscape? And who could clearly destroy us at any time, and did so in the past, but today observe the madness on planet Earth pretty dispassionately? Who are these types who manipulated us thousands of years ago and who even today give us a demonstration of technologies which can, for example, quite simply disable intercontinental missiles with nuclear warheads? That happened on March 24, 1967, at the site of the Oscar Flight Launch Control Facility in Montana.[63] None of the launch-ready missiles could be prepared for launch any longer. And this happened although each silo was located more than a kilometer from the next and each one had an independent power supply. Who is playing with us? Why do we have to put up with it? Are ETs really on Earth? Why could they do with us what they want—but are clearly refraining from doing so?

CHAPTER 3

WHO ARE THEY?
WHO ARE WE?

Where does life on our planet come from? I understood it when I was in high school. Life arose in the so-called "primordial soup" as proved by the famous experiments of Stanley Miller (1930–2007) and Harold Urey (1893–1981). In 1953, Miller, still a student at the University of California in Berkeley, started an experiment that had been suggested to him by his professor, Harold Urey. Miller and Urey introduced methane, water vapor, ammonia, carbon dioxide, and various minerals that existed billions of years ago on Earth into a sterile glass flask. Electrical sparks were fired into the experiment, and a week later, the first results were evident. Organic compounds were created, as well as amino acids, all of them the building blocks of life. The period in which a nutrient solution for primitive life could form out of the primordial soup is set by science at about 1.2 billion years. (A few million years either way are neither here nor there.) The Miller experiments were repeated several times under different conditions with varying results.[1] It has generally been assumed since Stanley Miller that life has arisen by itself, and all the more so as Stanley Miller received the backing of outstanding thinkers. The chemist Jacques Monod, former director of research in cell biology at the Pasteur Institute in Paris, wrote, "The old bond has broken; human beings finally know that they are alone in the indifferent expanses of the universe from which they emerged by accident."[2] And Professor Manfred Eigen, equally a Nobel Prize winner like his French colleague Jacques Monod, predicted as long ago as 1975, "It will be possible to reproduce every living creature artificially out of its natural genetic material, that is by other than natural means."[3] He was right. Today life forms are created by "non-natural means." It is, however, done from the natural genetic material. The physicist Jeremy England goes even further. He is convinced that every group of atoms would organize itself without external cause—that is, without lightning or electromagnetic waves. That would turn life into a logical sequence of physical laws. Coincidence would be out of the window and the universe should be teeming with life, because all matter consists of "groups of atoms" and they organize themselves, according to Jeremy England. Yet Jacques Monod contradicts this fascinating thought. He postulated, after all, that human beings were "*alone* in the expanses of the universe from which they emerged by accident."[4]

All in all, this is a picture that satisfied most scientists. It is the current orthodox view, multiplied a million times and set in concrete in all textbooks. Yet it is controversial: Atoms combine to form molecules. But collections of molecules are not life that propagates. In the long chain of chemical evolution the cell is the first, simplest life form. For that to arise, all the ingredients have to be present: amino acids, nucleic acids (formed from chains of nucleotides), and the basic building blocks adenine, guanine, cytosine, and thymine. These form the famous double-stranded structure of DNA (deoxyribonucleic acid), the double helix, and so on. (I don't want to bore my readers by writing a chapter about the chemical building blocks.)

The fact remains that in the first cell, which arose in the primordial soup, the complex molecular chain had to combine in the *correctly matching way*. A random collection of molecules, which happen to stick together, is not enough to form a cell. Neither is it any help to make the reciprocal magnetic effects that happen to exist on Earth responsible. A lock consists of a lock and a key. And the key has to fit into the lock. Only specific bases fit into the sequence of the double helix (DNA). Other basic building blocks *cannot* dock. And that raises the question: Why does it only work like this and not in any other way? Is there another program right from the beginning behind DNA or the innumerable other building blocks of life? Quite clearly they *can* only bond in a specific way. Specified by *what* or perhaps *whom*? Does something like "spirit in matter" exist, as the physicist Jean Charon put it?[5] Does what happens on Earth happen in the same way on other *earth-like* planets? And on Jupiter-like planets a different program is running that in turn only works there?

Chemical evolution, as I have just touched on it, is a firm part of our scientific thinking. Yet science is something living. Ways of looking at things other than what happens to be the dominant diktat force us to ask new questions. And there are indeed a number of clouds on the horizon.

The doubts already began to surface 44 years ago. At that time, the mathematician James Coppedege asked himself what the probability was that the chains of molecules would dock in the right position. After all, nothing happened in an orderly or, indeed, peaceful way in the primordial soup. It was fizzing, burning, and boiling. Toxic vapors dissolved everything again that might have come together. Mr. Coppedege played the following game: Our alphabet consists of 26 letters. If we wrote them on small cards, put them in a drum, and thoroughly mixed them up, the chance of fishing out the A would lie at 1:26. The word *evolution* consists of nine letters in a specific order. The probability of fishing these nine letters out of the drum in the correct sequence lies at 1:5,429,503,678,976.

Mr. Coppedege carried the game to extremes. He took the three words *evolution is impossible* as the subject of his calculations. The words consist of 21 letters and two spaces between the words. The chance of drawing the right letters in the right sequence out of the drum lies at 1:8,433,900,000, 000,000,000,000,000,000,000.

Now Mr. Coppedege proposed a machine that could draw a trillion letters out of the machine each second. In order to compose the words *evolution is impossible*, this utopian machine would have to rattle along for 26,000,000,000,000,000,000 years.[6]

That is all nonsense, the critics replied. Chemical evolution was not governed by the principle of chance but by *necessary* forms. Jacques Monod's *chance and necessity*.[7] Millions of molecules were swirling about in the primordial soup and would *have* to find themselves precisely where lock and key fitted together. This, in the opinion of the Nobel Prize winner Jacques Monod, happens of necessity. Today we say "without any alternative." Yet the permanent production of amino acids into enzymes and ultimately into proteins contradicts not only one, but two concrete laws of physics: the law of mass action and the law of entropy. Immense quantities of water opposed the microscopic amino acid particles. Here it should not be forgotten that amino acids are not living things; they cannot reproduce like cells, for example. Now the smallest "living" unit consists of at least 239 protein molecules. But a protein molecule itself is made up of 20 different amino acids and complex enzymes. To bring this confusing subject to a conclusion, the primordial soup, the "primordial atmosphere" in which this chemical game was played out, has no connection whatsoever with our atmosphere we breathe today. That primordial soup consisted primarily of methane and ammonia. Oxygen would have acted in this atmosphere like poison. If the first cells had been created in a methane-ammonia atmosphere, they would have been immediately killed off again by the addition of oxygen. Furthermore, all reactions leading to the formation of proteins are reversible. Chemicals forming by chance can dissolve again just as quickly. It has been proposed that the proteins did not form in the chaos of the primordial soup, but on the edges of craters: it was hot there; the proteins would have been destroyed.

The technical debate about chemical evolution rages unabated.[8,9,10] I have only briefly indicated the contradictions. In 1973, Francis Crick and Leslie Orgel, co-discoverers of the double helix structure of DNA, published an explosive article in the scientific journal *Icarus* entitled "Directed Panspermia."[11] In it, they postulate that an unknown alien intelligence had ensured that life in the universe would arise everywhere according to the same blueprint. The aliens had sent out a spaceship with various microorganisms.

> A payload of 1,000 kg might be made up of 10 samples each containing 10^{16} microorganisms, or 100 samples each of 10^{15} microorganisms. It would not be necessary to accelerate the spaceship to extremely high velocities, since its time of arrival would not be important. The radius of our galaxy is about 10^5 light years, so we could infect most planets in the galaxy within 10^8 yr by means of a spaceship traveling at only one-thousandth of the velocity of light. Several thousand stars are within a hundred light years of the Earth and could be reached within as little as a million years by a spaceship traveling at only 60,000 mph, or within 10,000 yr if a speed of one-hundredth of that of light were possible.[12]

Crick and Orgel thus shift the origin of life to a distant world. But there the same problems had to be overcome as with us. This problem preoccupied the Swedish physicist and Nobel Prize winner Savante Arrhenius (1859–1927) as long as 80 years ago. Somewhere, he writes, life must have started, and he postulates that life was eternal, thereby avoiding the question about its origin.[13] Of course, even a circular line had to start somewhere, but as soon as the circle was closed the question as to its beginning no longer arose. It could no longer be answered. Behind the start, some kind of "creation," or what the religions describe as "God," had to be assumed.

Why can the start of the circle not have been the Earth? Because it simply does not work *chronologically*. This has been clearly shown by the astrophysicists Sir Fred Hoyle, the mathematics genius Chandra Wickramasinghe, and the Nobel Prize winner Francis Crick. Their works are full of mathematical equations that all lead to the same conclusion: life did not arise on Earth because the *time* for its development with the myriad coincidences needed for the creation of the molecular chains was in no instance enough.[14, 15, 16, 17]

In the summer of 1980, a scientific congress at the Hebrew University in Jerusalem concerned itself with the question: Did Adam come from space?[18] This is Professor Wolmann on the subject:

> We know from chemical analyses that the fundamental building blocks of life are chemical compounds with monster molecules. Each of these molecules consists of several hundred thousand to millions of atoms. We call these chemical substances polymers.... We think that the

basic substances from which nature created the first polymers did not come from earth but from space.

These arguments should actually be enough: Life did not start with us. One competent crown witness is still missing: Professor Bruno Vollmert (1920–2002). Vollmert was professor of molecular chemistry at the University of Karlsruhe. He concerned himself intensively both with chemical and Darwinian evolution. At the end of his many years of research, he admitted:

> DNA and thus life could not arise by itself...but since, on the other hand, life has always clearly been there, so that also pieces of DNA (genes) can be analyzed and recreated at any time in the laboratory, it must either always have existed (which is not the case) or it owes its existence to intelligent, purposeful planning, is the result of planned design....[19]

Vollmert displayed moral courage. He accused his colleagues of "ideological motives" and slew them with precise calculations:

> The probability of realizing one of ten assumed intermediate stages, to be on the safe side, of the growth curve of DNA through statistical copolymerization on the path to a new class of living creature is 1:10 to the power of 4,000. The only honest interpretation of this probability is that Darwin's theory of the origin of species and life

as such through mutation and selection was and is a big misapprehension.[20]

Chandra Wickramasinghe, holder of several doctorates, is currently the director of the Buckingham Centre for Astrobiology of the University of Buckingham in England. He is considered to be a mathematical genius and has received honors worldwide in the field of mathematics. At a congress in Sindelfingen town hall in the spring of 2015, he analyzed the impossibility of chemical evolution in front of an audience of 3,000 people.[21] He told me personally at dinner, "You can forget the story with the primordial soup. It was a good thought—but total nonsense."

With such an accumulation of scholarly statements, all of them made by top scientists, we have to ask ourselves: Why does the old doctrine still apply? Why are students in high schools and universities not taught the two different opinions? The motive is what it has always been: ideology. The one group denies both god and extraterrestrials. In its eyes, we human beings are the only ones in the universe. The faithful in all religions have been taught that we are the crown of creation, students of science that we are the pinnacle of evolution. In both cases, be it religion or science, there is only one valid insight: we are the greatest. A being like God has, in any case, been abolished for a long time. It never fit in with human self-importance.

Chemical evolution did not take place on Earth. Period. The building blocks of life came from outside. Who sent them? Are those legendary "forefathers" the same who visited the Earth thousands of years ago? Or the descendants of those "forefathers"? The same who show themselves through UFOs? Who kidnap individual people and create marvelous pictures in the corn and wheat fields? And if it is them, what is it all about? What do "they" get out of it? And what about Darwinian evolution? Darwin's evolutionary theory is the credo of anthropology. In scientific circles, it is downright sacrilegious not to believe in it. Everyone who doubts Darwin's theory is an ignorant bore who can be ignored. Yet hardly a year passes without another press conference at which even more recent discoveries about the human race are announced. The fossil concerned is then deemed to be the most recent prehistoric human being—until the next event of this kind.

All life-forms develop from genes. What actually is such a gene? Professor Beda Stadler, geneticist at the University of Bern, explains it:

> Genes can be described as precisely defined sections of DNA which represent the blueprint for RNA molecules from which proteins are created.... All genes together are called the genome.... In higher living organisms, the genome exists in several strings which are packaged separately and are called chromosomes. All chromosomes in turn are packaged in the cell nucleus. In human beings the whole set of chromosomes in each nucleated cell consists of 46 chromosomes, whereby 23 come from the mother and 23 from the father.[22]

Clear?

The genetic code is the key to every life form. Anyone who knows this code can manipulate any living creature as they like by changing the basic sequence in the DNA spiral. The whole thing started in 1973, when the biologists Stanley Cohen and Herbert Boyer succeeded for the first time in implanting a foreign gene into a bacterium. Today it is commonplace. Every geneticist knows how it is done. At the time of our grandfathers, it was still "grafting": certain characteristics of a plant are transferred to another one. Such things are everyday occurrences for biologists and no one gets excited about them. In genetics, the procedure is different: The nucleus of a cell is stripped out, and the chemical building blocks in the DNA string (the double helix) are moved to another location in the string and reintroduced into the cell. But beforehand the geneticist must know *where* he want to change *what* and what the result should be. The cell nucleus can also be removed and implanted in the cell of another living organism. That procedure is called "cloning" and is always done with cells of *the same* animal species. Dolly the sheep was created in this way in 1997, a 100-percent copy of the donor animal. Dolly has long since given birth to healthy offspring. Then, in the spring of 2008, the British government permitted the creation of hybrid creatures, so-called "chimeras." Here the nucleus is taken from the cells of *different* living organisms, a cow and a human being, for example, and the human cell nucleus injected into the empty cell of the cow. A short electrical impulse stimulates the cell to divide and the cow cell multiplies with the genetic information

of the human being. Insane? Nature has done this for millions of years. Without human intervention. A so-called
"retrovirus" such as the AIDS virus penetrates a cell, copies
its own genetic information, and multiplies. The Australian
geneticist Andrew Pask from the University of Melbourne
implanted the genome of a Tasmanian tiger into a mouse
embryo and got the cells to multiply.[23] Similar experiments
are being undertaken worldwide. The aim is genetic modi-
fication, superficially the "improvement of human beings."
Defects such as Alzheimer's or multiple sclerosis are to be
eradicated through such "therapeutic cloning."

As long ago as 1987, Japanese geneticists developed a
so-called "super sequencer," which daily decoded a million
"letters" of DNA. That was just the beginning. The U.S. geneticist Craig Venter wanted to reveal the "transparent human
being," that is, the complete human genome. He has meanwhile succeeded in doing so—with some complications. In
his most recent bombshell, Craig Venter announced that his
scientific team had developed a miniature life form. In other
words, a living "thing." Made by human beings. Uncanny!
The life form consists of 531,560 letters of DNA and is desig-
nated "Syn3.0." Although this synthetic thing is alive, Craig
Venter does not know why, either.[24] More than 480 genes
were implanted, others were removed.

Until a few months ago (I write these words in the summer of 2016), such artificial modifications to the human genome were considered to be a highly complex laboratory act.
Swapping individual genes could take months and, furthermore, was very expensive. Meanwhile everything has become

simple. Kathy Niakan, geneticist at the London Francis Crick Institute, the French microbiologists Emmanuelle Charpentier, and Jennifer Dudna developed a new method of modifying the genome with pinpoint accuracy. The procedure is called CRISPR-CAS9 technique. What is almost like a molecular pair of scissors made of the protein CAS9 is used which, similar to a virus, cuts through the DNA string at precisely the desired place.[25] It is a surgical procedure on the genome—"genome editing." "CRISPR works like child's play," the German news magazine *Der Spiegel* quotes the German geneticist Rudolf Jaenisch.[26]

People who have no idea about what happens inside a cell rant about genetically modified food and warn with a wagging finger against everything connected with genetics. They don't know that the enzymes in quite ordinary washing powders were cooked up in the genetic kitchen. Just like lecithin, which occurs in hundreds of foodstuffs. It comes from genetically modified soybeans. The same applies to the glucose syrup that is added to all kinds of drinks. To make glucose syrup, an enzyme is required "which today comes almost exclusively from genetically modified organisms."[27]

And now we have the CRISPR-CAS9 technique. With this genetic weapon, the targeted control of evolution becomes a fact—any time, be it in the past or the future. Animals, humans, and anything else growing on Earth can be modified quickly and easily. Presumably the ETs have mastered not just the CRISPR procedure but even more sophisticated methods of artificially mutating life forms. Did they do that? Can rifts or completely paradoxical modifications be shown in biological evolution that cannot be explained by natural means? Was Charles Darwin with his *Origin of the Species*[28] fundamentally right—but not always? After all, he couldn't at his time know about the genetic code, much less about artificial mutations.

There are indeed living creatures on our blue planet whose existence raises huge questions. For example, 4,000 meters down in the deep ocean where luminous monsters developed in absolute darkness, including a creature called a pistol shrimp, which does away with its opponents using boiling hot water. Or the ischnochiton, a primitive sea animal that has a carapace made of eight superimposed plates. On the upper plate there are hundreds of tiny eyes hidden in small hollows. In this way, the animal can see everything in its surroundings. Each tiny eye has its own sensory organ. A total contradiction to evolution. Even more fantastical, there are species of beetles with weapons that could not have arisen by natural means. One is of a very special kind: the bombardier beetle. They frighten or kill their enemies with a highly toxic secretion that sprays out from a combustion chamber in the abdomen at around 100 degrees Celsius. This secretion consists of the chemicals hydroquinone and hydrogen peroxide with the addition of the enzymes catalase and peroxidase. A catalyst is created that mixes the chemicals into toxic benzoquinone (detonating gas). This detonating gas explodes and sprays at its target out of the body of the bombardier beetle. It does so at a temperature of 100 degrees Celsius.[29, 30] In the whole process, the chemicals involved enter the combustion chamber through a very thin valve. After each explosion, the

Milk Hill,
Alton Barnes,
Wiltshire, UK.
June 21, 2009.

Smeathes Plantation,
near Ogbourne, Down
Gallop, Wiltshire, UK.
July 24, 2009.

Badbury Rings,
near Wimborne
Minster, Dorset, UK.
June 17, 2014.

Cheesefoot Head, near
Winchester, Hampshire, UK.
August 9, 2012.

Avebury Trusloe, UK.
July 22, 2000.

Roundway Hill, near Devizes, Wiltshire, UK. July 25, 2010.

Windmill Hill, near Avebury, Wiltshire, UK. July 26, 2011.

White Sheet Hill, near Mere, Wiltshire, UK. June 25, 2010.

Chipping, Haselor, Warwickshire, UK. July 20, 2015.

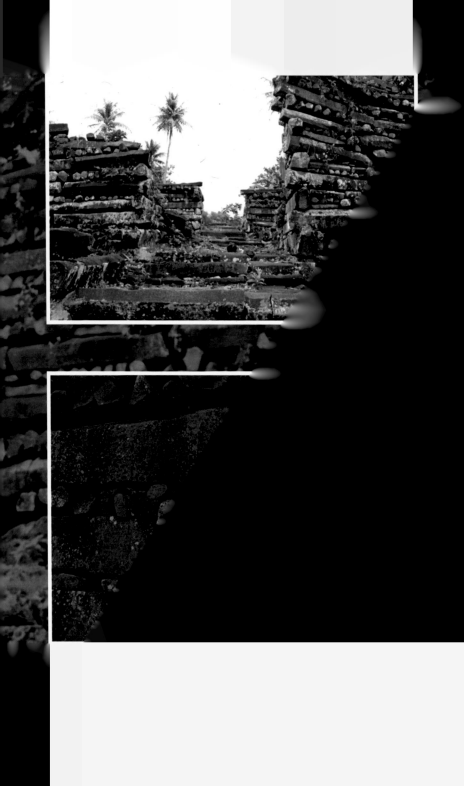

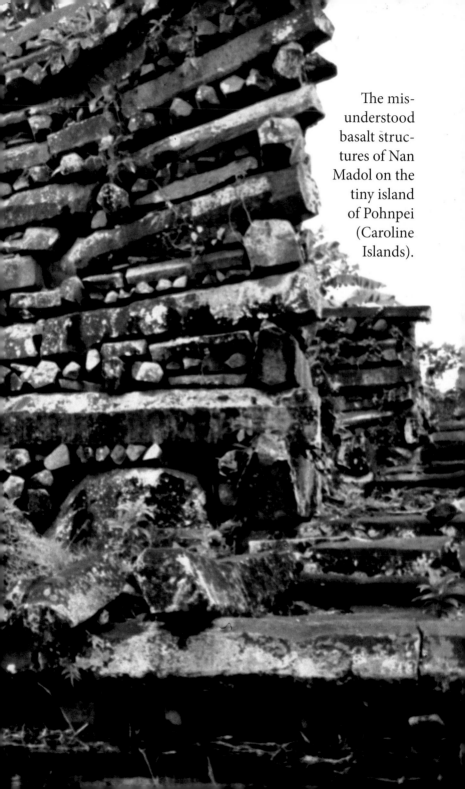

The misunderstood basalt structures of Nan Madol on the tiny island of Pohnpei (Caroline Islands).

Stained glass window of the Miracle of the Sun in the Basilica of Fatima, Portugal.

Basalt stairs at the Gunung Padang site, Java, Indonesia.

Galaxy image source: NASA and STScI.

chamber is closed with a flap, which opens again for the next explosion. Two tiny reflectors—one on each side—enable the bombardier beetle to shoot round corners. It kills not just small attackers but also toads, which are a hundred times bigger.

How is this weapon in the body of the beetle supposed to have developed slowly? The wall of the combustion chamber consists of a resistant coating of proteins and chitin. The toxic mixture shoots out of a controllable spray gland in the abdomen. The reflectors can guide the poisonous jet around corners. How are the chemical components supposed to have developed in the body, slowly from generation to generation? Did the combustion chamber already exist or was it created later on? The controllable jet? The reflectors? Did everything develop at the same time? Willy-nilly in a beetle family? And the combustion chamber with its two valves? It must already have been present when the chemical developed—however that may have happened. Otherwise the beetle itself would have exploded when the chemicals mixed. Evolution cut short. And the tiny flap that opens rapidly before each deadly shot and immediately closes again? And then there is still the beetle's brain. Coupled with its sensory organs, the chemicals have to be instructed to mix now, at lightning speed when an enemy appears. And the firing gland must be pointed at the opponent like a gun barrel. Then the command to fire.

All a bit hard to swallow. Through which commands, which "spirit," are the individual parts of this weapon supposed to have come together? Did the beetle tell its body, "I need a combustion chamber, a jet, a gun flap that opens and closes at lightning speed? Two external reflectors made of very durable material?" After all, they not only have to stand the acids but also 100 degree temperatures. A slow development extending over generations does not work here. Now I am not of the opinion that some "gods" somewhere had interfered with the beetle genome and created the beetle's weapons, but I think it is conceivable that the beetle was imported from an alien world. Even if it was not in a completely finished state, then at least its genome, similar to snakes or rats that get to remote islands on ships.

The beetle is tiny, the whale huge. Every school student learns that whales are mammals and originally lived on the land. That also applies to other marine mammals. So at some point in its development, the original whale must have plopped into the water. Perhaps it also waddled in unhurriedly because it became too hot outside. Then it loses its feet, forms flippers, mates under water, and also suckles its young in the wet element. Where have the hydraulics of the extendable underwater nipples come from? They must have been there from the beginning, otherwise the juvenile would have perished immediately after birth. And in general the question applies: If all of this was of benefit to the life form concerned—survival of the fittest—why did others of the same species not do the same?

There is no dispute: Mutation (changes) constantly takes place within a species. I read somewhere that there are said to be a thousand different species of spiders. All of them are related to one another, and have a common spider ancestor. And the latter in turn has descended from I know not what miniature monster. But a spider will not turn into a cow, not after hundreds of millions of years. The first vertebrates are said to have emerged from worm species. And at some point a living clump of cells mutated into a crab. This now has to mate to continue the evolutionary chain. With *whom* should he mate? Did the random mutation that created the crab affect a whole horde? We mammals are said to have originated from bony fish. The fish mutated and the swim bladder could no longer obtain oxygen from the water but from the air. The lung was born. From these "coelacanths" it was only a small step to the first amphibian. Great! And what did this amphibian get up to in its endless solitude? It developed into a crawler, a mammal, and so on. They now laid their eggs on dry land. At some point the first reptile developed, which could, however, no longer pair with its relative, the amphibians. New fellow creatures of the same species with the same number of chromosomes were required and they were— what a surprise!—suddenly available.

What is the origin of these changes? The genes are responsible, they are the most important data medium, "but they are only a small link in the complex and fascinating chains of life."[31] There is no dispute that we are the closest relatives to the apes. Until a few years ago, it was said that our genes were 99 percent identical with those of the great apes. We had the same ancestors, the same skeleton, and the same protein structure. In the non-stop series of thousands and thousands of mutations over millions of years, quite a few things have changed from the ancestor of the apes to us—only the proteins haven't. Comparatively, the differences between the protein forms of two frogs are 50 times greater than those between chimpanzees and humans. Professor Alan C. Wilson and his colleague Mary-Claire King, both biochemists from the University of California who showed these divergences in the proteins of frogs, say, "There must be a hitherto undiscovered and much more effective evolutionary motor than we know of so far."[32]

Now Dr. Marie-Laure Yaspo from the Max Planck Institute for Molecular Genetics in Berlin has informed the public that the differences between humans and chimpanzees were, after all, greater than thought. I quote:

> So far it has been assumed that humans and chimpanzees only differed slightly in their genome. But now a team of scientists from Germany, China, Japan, Korea and Taiwan has discovered in a direct comparison of the chimpanzee chromosome 22 and its human equivalent, chromosome 21, *that in the human genome there were almost 68,000 insertions or deletions.* [Author's italics] While most of these changes have no or only a slight influence on the function of the coded proteins, the researchers nevertheless found in 20 percent of them significant structural differences. If these differences are extrapolated to the whole genome, *apes and humans could differ in several thousand genes*—which

would better explain the differences between both species.[33]

The scientific findings are dynamite—and no one seems to notice. The evolutionary distance between humans and mice is said to be 60 million years. Between chimpanzees and humans it is perhaps two or three million. Now, believe it or not, 68,000 longer differing segments were found in the genome between humans and chimpanzees. *"Yet this means that the amino acid sequence of the 231 discovered coded proteins in humans and apes varies by 83 percent."*[34] (Author's italics) Why, who, or what caused this gigantic mutation? We are not talking about 50 or 100 random mutations in the genome, but 68,000. They were not inserted or deleted at random by nature—whatever that may be. The differences are targeted.

What are we? Fundamentally a product of evolution. But why are we so different from our genetically related apes? The primate researcher Frans de Waal from Emory University in Atlanta thinks that language differentiates us fundamentally from the apes because human survival depends on it.[35] According to this logic, we would not exist without language. No, say other scientists. It was our social behavior that constituted our humanity, as if a troop of gorillas, a school of dolphins, or a pride of lions did not possess any social behavior.

"We are bastards," Professor David Reich from the Massachusetts Institute of Technology in Cambridge tells us.[36] The lines of humans and chimpanzees had already been divided the far side of Eden, then the two species had subsequently exchanged genes between one another again. "After pre-humans had already lived for hundreds of thousands of years as an own species, they suddenly started engaging in sexual intercourse with their knuckle-walking relatives again."[37]

Nothing is impossible, but why would an upright, walking hominid suddenly spurn a fellow member of his species and have sex with a fur-covered ape? Furthermore, the product of such love would be a genetically retrograde step. The bastard would not have better genes, quite apart from the question as to whether the chromosomes of human and chimpanzee would be compatible in the first place.

The heretical thoughts I put forward are not in principle directed against evolution. We are quite simply offshoots of apes and all dumb cows are related to one another. A "primordial mother spider" probably exists somewhere and all insects, the stinging and the harmless ones, are descended from a sticky conglomerate of cells. But I have good reason to reject the extraordinary amalgamation of species with the inexpressibly complex changes of the molecular chain. Scholars such as the Nobel Prize winner Sir Francis Crick, the astrophysicist Chandra Wickramasinghe, or Bruno Vollmert, professor of molecular chemistry, are neither amateurs nor idiots. Professor Olivier Mühlemann, University of Bern, a brilliant representative of biochemistry, writes, "How did life arise? Plausible answers to this question, which is of such key importance for the way we see ourselves and our worldview, have been supplied in the last 200 years above all by the sciences—with Charles Darwin leading the way with his simple and elegant *evolutionary theory which has been confirmed x-thousandfold. It explains coherently how today's diversity of living creatures developed out of common, identical primordial cells.*" (Author's italics)[38] There is not the slightest doubt for the learned professor, neither about chemical nor Darwinian evolution (...*confirmed x-thousandfold...it explains coherently...*).

But why, then, does Professor Vollmert (and others) say the precise opposite? "(The cell)...*owes its existence to intelligent, purposeful planning...Darwin's theory about the origin of species...was and is a great misapprehension.*"[39] (Author's italics)

All professors are upright, highly intelligent scholars and yet they reach completely different views. And this is multiplied a hundred times because there are at least a hundred book titles by thoroughly honest scientists *against* evolution. Important intellects among them, such as Dr. Thomas Nagel, currently professor of philosophy at the University of California, and those at Berkley and Princeton. Professor Nagel uncovered a number of fundamental contradictions that argue *against* current evolutionary theory.[40] Since then he has been under fire from his colleagues. Why, oh why, do scientists, who often went to the same schools, fight one another so vehemently?

The catchword is always *ideology.* The pro-Darwin faction is reviled as materialists, the opposing school dismissed as creationists who still believe in a god. Yet god means nothing at all to many who hold views against evolution. Opinions are entrenched and judgments have been made. Such behavior in science is no different to religion or ideology. The one side doesn't even bother to read the books of the other side. Each group insists that it is right. And each group looks with pity on the other which "simply refuses to see sense." The pioneer Craig Venter believed he had decoded the human genome, made the "transparent human being" visible. Then clever geneticists found that there is no generally valid genome. For genes do not just work by themselves. They are always active in association with hundreds of other genes. The idea that genes are lined up on a string like pearls is deceptive. "All the genetic material contains overlapping information," confirms Dr. Roderic Guigo from the Centre for Genome Regulation in Barcelona.[41]

And these busy researchers keep coming across things that are impossible, things that can be proved but should not exist. Such "impossible things" appear briefly, cause irritation, and are immediately dumped back in the chamber of forgetfulness. What kind of things?

In 1960, several stone tools were found near Hueyatlaco, 120 kilometers southeast of Mexico City. They were dated by four different methods: 1) uranium dating, 2) fission track dating, 3) tephra hydration, and 4) mineral weathering. All methods produced an age of about 250,000 years. Impossible for the evolutionists. There could not be any human tools 250,000 years ago. Michael Cremo and Richard Thomson, both scientists, wrote in their thoroughly researched book *Forbidden Archaeology*:

> ...the problem lies much deeper than Hueyatlaco. It concerns the manipulation of scientific thinking through the suppression of puzzling data. Data which call the currently prevailing way of thinking into question.... Our work in Hueyatlaco was rejected by most archaeologists because it contradicts the theory. Their argumentation is circular. Homo sapiens sapiens developed in Eurasia about 30–50,000 years ago. Hence it is impossible that there are tools which are 250,000 years old which can be traced back to Homo sapiens sapiens since Homo sapiens sapiens did not arise until about 30,000 years ago, etc. Such a way of thinking produces self-satisfied scientists but lousy science![42]

Cremo and Thompson, the latter a mathematician at Cornell University in Ithaca, New York, give several well-documented examples from the Pliocene (5.3 to 2.5 million years ago) and the Miocene, which lies up to 23 million years in the past. They are always bones, objects which have no business in the period concerned, but clearly exist.[43] At Bruniquel Cave in southern France, there is also a stone circle with a diameter of about six meters. It was dated by archaeologists from the University of Bordeaux to 176,000 years. Definitively and unalterably. So someone acted purposefully 176,000 years ago. Neanderthals? And why? Things become even more confusing: Bones were found in a cave in the Altai Mountains (the borderland of Mongolia and Siberia) and analyzed at the Max Planck Institute for Evolutionary Anthropology in Leipzig: "The clearly human bones from the Denisova Cave do not match the human genome. The genome of the Denisova human differs more than twice as much from the one of Homo sapiens than the one from Neanderthals."[44]

These are by no means isolated cases, but hundreds of contradictory findings that the one side chucks in the waste-paper bin with irritation.

As long as 40 years ago[45] and thereafter I introduced a thought to the discussion, which is today becoming more and more realistic: specific, artificial, external mutation. The Christian world is generally familiar with the "virgin birth." Mary, the mother of Jesus, is said to have conceived immaculately from the "Holy Spirit." The story is not, of course, true, as I have also shown.[46] But where does this idea of artificial insemination come from? In the Old Testament, such miracles are described in several places. The infertile women Sarah (Gen. 18:10–14) and Rebecca (Gen. 25:21–26), and in Samuel (1 Sam. 2–5), and so on, all experienced the happiness of having been visited by some heavenly beings just like Melchizedek, the king of Salem. But this "seed from heaven" was actually something quite normal in the ancient Orient. Every ruler had to be of "divine descent," otherwise he wasn't worth a great deal. The Egyptian god Amun-Re mated with the mothers of the heirs to the throne. Alexander the Great

(356–323 BC) is said to have been conceived through a lightning bolt. The Assyrian king Ashurbanipal (668–622) was
a son of the goddess Ishtar. Allegedly. Anyhow, he founded a magnificent library of clay tablets. The Akkadian king
Hammurabi (1728–1686 BC) also belonged to the heavenly births. His mother was made pregnant by the sun god.
Hammurabi is known for the oldest written code of law:
Hammurabi's Code. Religious figures such as Buddha or
Zarathustra were also begot through a "divine ray" in the
body of their virgin mothers, just like the founder of the
Tibetan empire, Gesar, or the first emperors of China. The
same applies to the original rulers of the Incas and Aztecs.
The motif is ancient and, we might say, international. In
the Babylonian Gilgamesh epic, which goes back to Sumer,
Gilgamesh, king of the city of Uruk, was created by the
gods Shamash and Hadad: "Thus the great gods created
Gilgamesh: eleven cubits high he was...two thirds god, one
third man."[47]

It really becomes fantastical with the mutations practiced by the so-called gods on hybrid beings, the chimeras
which are said to have existed at least in the tales of the ancient chroniclers:

> They also begat human beings with two wings;
> furthermore, human beings with goat's legs and
> horns on their heads; and still others with horses'
> hooves, and others in the shape of a horse at the
> rear and a human shape at the front...they also

made bulls with human heads...as well as other
monsters...[48]

This is how the Church Father Eusebius described it, who
has entered church history as the Bishop of Caesarea and as
a chronicler (died 339 AD). Eusebius quotes extensively from
the works of the Egyptian historian Manetho. He in turn is
mentioned in the Greek historian Plutarch as a contempo-
rary of the first Ptolomaean king (304–282 BC). And what
do Manetho/Eusebius say? That there had been hybrid creatures of horse and human? The centaur says hello! Bulls with
human heads? Didn't one of those live in the labyrinth on
Crete?

For us rationally thinking people, there are only two alternatives with regard to hybrid creatures: all of it ignorant
fantasy, or genetic design. Logically, chimeras cannot have
arisen naturally. The numbers of chromosomes of the monsters do not fit with one another. *If* they existed at any time,
then only by artificial mutation of the DNA string. Who
mastered this technique thousands of years ago?

One can take the view that all these handed-down stories
of heavenly births, divine kings, or hybrid creatures were a
product of our ancestors' imagination. They *wished for* something like that. But that is too easy. The oldest writings come
from Sumer, cuneiform writing, and a little later from Egypt,
the hieroglyphs. The first scribes, who, with some kind of
stylus, produced thicker or thinner lines on their clay tablets,
were no science fiction writers. Writing was deemed to be a
high art. Only a few mastered it. Yet in our time, we assume

that these original scribes had entrusted fantasy tales to their clay tablets. I suggest that the rulers or high priests of the time would never have permitted such an abuse. The truth was communicated. Why on Earth, then, did they write, "Thus the great gods created Gilgamesh: eleven cubits high he was...two thirds god, one third man."[49]

In our time, there have been new translations from a completely new perspective and they produce a totally different picture from before. I have already referred to the translation by Dr. Hermann Burgard.[50] Dr. Burgard is a specialist in Sumerian characters. He knows every root word, every cross connection, every interpretation, and every previous work on the subject by his colleagues from the school of Sumerology. Now he has tackled the texts of the high priestess Enheduanna. She scribbled cuneiform on many tables 4,300 years ago. Dr. Burgard accuses his colleagues of sticking with the misapprehensions of decades. On the basis of these ancient texts, Burgard proves the former existence of a space station in orbit. This space habitat was reached from Earth "with a smaller machine." That in turn docked in a landing bay which "closed like a trap."[51, 52] The previous translations, undertaken by honorable scholars, are shown to be erroneous because they start from false premises. Thinking in a different zeitgeist. In that far distant past of humanity, Dr. Burgard says, it was not some heaven full of bliss which was sung about, not some meteorological phenomenon or natural disaster which was described. At no time was it about diffuse religions or psychological nonsense but hard reality.

The same—that is how I interpret it—applies to the texts about "heavenly births" and hybrid beings. Even if an extraterrestrial birth might have been imputed to many a king or religious leader after the event, some of these genetically modified forms did actually exist. They were intended to guide humanity—the masses—in a new direction. These mutations were created without exception by the alleged "gods," the ETs. Why for heaven's sake? And how can it be proved?

The proof has to be provided by the geneticists, and it should not even be that difficult. But where is the recognized expert with sufficient courage to go public? As soon as even just one *artificial* mutation can be proved in the past, the same rules apply as do with regard to the SETI censorship. With such evidence, it is not just the existence of ETs that is proved, but also their influence on human society. In any event, I can confirm that these thousands-of-years-old traditions repeatedly report about human beings who were conceived by artificial insemination. There is a clear statement of this in the Lamech scroll, one of the Dead Sea Scrolls. (I have already reported several times about it.) There we can learn that the seed of Noah was placed in the lap of Bat Enosh, Noah's mother, by the "heavenly watchers."[53] Now, and everyone knows it, we are all supposed to be the descendants of Noah. Never mind what name the guy might have been given in other cultures.

This means that all of humanity carries extraterrestrial genes within it. What was that about the 68,000 differences between the human and chimpanzee genome? "Yet this means that the amino acid sequence of the 231 discovered coded proteins in humans and apes varies by 83 percent.[54]

We are indeed products of evolution—but not only. Why, however, must an 81-year-old writer who is not a geneticist point out these connections in our society? Because I am familiar with the connections from the traditions handed down in humanity—that is, what others are lacking. Also, some experts know very well what I know but are not allowed to write about it because of their professional ethics.

The mother of all questions remains: *Why?* What will extraterrestrials gain from producing intelligent human beings from an ape species; repeatedly making outstanding leaders over the millennia; showing themselves in the form of UFOs, or, indeed, creating magnificent pictures in our fields? None of that makes any sense. Where is the context?

Have you ever thought about ants? There are about 13,000 (thirteen thousand!) different species and worldwide presumably billions of the little creatures. There are safari ants, which do not build any nests but march about. There are myrmicinae, formicines, black and red ants, forest ants, bigger and smaller animals. There are said to be carpenter ants or weaver ants, which build their nests from leaves. There are ant hills in trees and leafcutter ants, which break down leaves and carry them into the nest. Mainly in the Amazon, there are even mixed colonies that engage in a regular slave trade and make the ants they capture work for them. Then there are varieties such as the white and red termites. All of them live in perfectly organized states with queens, soldiers, scouts, and workers.

Normally, ant colonies are organized by castes. Each group is responsible for a different task, such as construction, food, parental care, or protection of the structure. The females actually establish the nests. They lay thousands of eggs; the rest of the colony serves to protect and bring up the young. The termites, particularly the dampwood termites and Rhinotermitidiae, are very inventive. Their structures consist of a maze of passages that lead toward the inside to the "royal chamber" and toward the outside to proper covered "access roads." Ventilation in the building is perfect, neither too hot nor too cold. There are "fermenting chambers," "mushroom cultures," and even proper "guest rooms," for certain types of ants keep beetles as guests. They feed them and benefit from their secretions. Ant colonies engage in proper warfare against one another. Then scouts are sent out, and they spy and inform on one another. Treacherous attacks are commonplace. Foreign queens are disrespectfully cut into pieces, and workers are forced to work as slaves in the nest. This and many other things prove that there is a lot of experience in each ant state, but also memory and the ability to identify and communicate.

Do ants know who or what humans are?

Stand before an ant hill and let the little creatures run up and down you. The ants will still not be aware of what a human is. This is how our memory, our technology, our consciousness works. The little animals can stare into our car headlights, hear the noise of our civilization, register our exhaust gases. They will still not recognize us. Gently place the animal into a glass, photograph it on your kitchen table, and then carry the ant back to its hill. The little creature will now run about excitedly calling out, "I was kidnapped by an extra-ant intelligence." But all its fellow ants will of course know that there is *no* extra-ant intelligence. The kidnapped animal is shunned, suffers from depression, and can no longer be happy. No one believes it. Even its closest friends turn away. "What were you thinking?" they complain. "Do you think you're something special? Even if there is some extra-ant intelligence out there, why would they choose you in particular? They would have contacted our scouts or our queen directly...."

Can you see the scale of this? We humans could learn ant language in a special training program and teach them to consume other foods than they do at present. It would also be within our power to end ant wars. After all, each war leads to the torture and dismemberment of ants; suffering, exclusion, the destruction of nests, refugees who no longer have a home and fear for their life. Why don't we humans stop the ant wars? How can we watch such terrible slaughter without doing something?

Because we don't care a jot about what happens in ant colonies.

And the extraterrestrials in relationship to us? Quite clearly they *do* care a jot what happens with us. They do observe our wars, although they have the means to stop them at any time. (Have you forgotten the disabled intercontinental missiles of March 24, 1967, at the Flight Launch Control

Facility in Montana?) The ETs do not interfere in our politics, although they often smell to high heaven. They don't kidnap or punish dictators, or reveal themselves on public screens or above football stadiums. Indeed, they don't enslave humanity. So what do they want? Why the interest in us?

The whole of the universe is inconceivably large. At least for human understanding. Just as astrophysics posits a Big Bang (or several big bangs) in the beginning, so philosophy (or religion) likes to see an "original God" at the start. Plus and minus. Ying and Yang. The Big Bang creates matter, the "original God" spirit or information. With regard to the "Big Bang," we do not yet know with certainty whether the universe is expanding forever or whether it will at some point collapse again. *Information*, on the other hand, strives for infinitude until the whole universe is filled with information (intelligence). Every nook and cranny of space is to become "divine." The exchange of information is to take place through all dimensions, periods, and parallel worlds. That requires the spread of intelligence. It has to infiltrate matter with "spirit." This process takes place through the multiplication of intelligent beings. No intelligence exists without curiosity. It is the trigger of proliferation. That is why the original extraterrestrial intelligence makes sure that life can arise everywhere. That is how the universe is infected with the building blocks of life—the bewildering chains of molecules that only fit together like a key into a lock.

Life, and thus evolution, arises on every suitable planet. From this, the most fantastic forms can in turn grow: crocodiles, grasshoppers, dinosaurs, elephants, and birds. But evolution also knows *mandatory forms.* Only species with the right instruments increase intelligence. Thus for creatures living in the water, it is impossible to invent electricity or the computer. Or metals can only be mixed with heat and turned into alloys. Furthermore, chains of molecules *can only* be made visible under an electron microscope—an impossible discovery for snakes or crocodiles. Evolution is full of *mandatory developments.* They are already contained in the building blocks of life. The development into apes was no accident; there was no alternative.

Now advanced extraterrestrial intelligences will probably have knowledge of more sophisticated astronomical processes than we do. They will know which suns are orbited by which planets, know which planets are in the habitable zone. Only now, after evolution has been at work for millions of years, are spaceships sent out. Not randomly, but to the specific places where life *must have developed.* When the aliens came to our earth we already had millions of species, including our ancestors, the apes. The ETs caught a number of them, changed the base sequence in the DNA molecule, and implanted the mutated cell into the womb of a female chimpanzee. A fetus might also have been grown in vitro (in the test tube) as a test-tube baby. After the gestation period, the female gave birth to a baby with the same skeleton, the same skull, the same physique, the same immunoreactions— but with *additional* hereditary factors that chimpanzees did not have. Curiosity, the capacity for language = information exchange. There was a sense of culture, such as for sculpture, music, painting, religion, and the most important of all, technology. From today's perspective, it made sense to screen the first humans from the environment and place them in a "Garden of Eden." After all, the first humans—let's call them Adam and Eve—did not master any language. From their ancestors they only knew grunts and sibilants. The language of the first generation of humans was the language of the gods. This assumption is today still reflected in the tradition of the Tower of Babel: "And the whole earth was of one language, and of one speech." (Genesis 11:1)

The day came when "the gods" left for other solar systems to create further intelligence there. On their departure the following might have happened: The first humans knelt before the aliens. The latter said, "We are no gods. We are of the same flesh and blood as you. Never create an image of God because God is intangible and undefinable." The continuation of this imagined conversation can be read in Moses: "Be fruitful, and multiply, and replenish the earth, and subdue it: and have dominion over the fish of the sea, and over the fowl of the air, and over every living thing that moveth upon the earth." (Genesis 1:28)

The instruction was clear: Intelligent life was to multiply and rule over non-intelligent life forms. But there was one crucial commandment that the first humans must never break: They must no longer engage in sexual intercourse with their non-intelligent fellow members of the species. This would have been genetically regressive. But it happened immediately. Someone carried on with a non-mutated fellow member of the species. This entered human memory as "original sin." The calamity started. When the "gods" returned centuries later, "it repented the Lord that he had made man on the earth, and it grieved him at his heart." (Genesis 6:6–8) The Flood was decided, the experiment was abandoned, and a new one was started. The father of humanity after the Flood was called Noah—other cultures called him by different names. And he in turn was a figure begotten by the "watchers in the sky." Since Noah, we humans are no longer purely Earth beings. Changed genes are a part of our genome.

Humanity grew, spread over the earth, developed various languages and cultures. The constant disputes between the groups led each tribe to develop its own weapons and better methods of defense. War may not be the father of all things, but the source of quite a lot of technology.

Why were there wars in the first place? Could the ETs not have prevented them? The exchange of information among humans means that it was almost *inevitable* that different opinions formed. The independence of mind, the pride of human beings led them to believe that only their own view was the correct one. The "gods" could have dissipated the tension and thus presumably created a peaceful, totally boring society. This, in turn, would have failed through laziness. In a life without tension, people seek to increase pleasure. This means their grey cells aren't exercised a great deal. We *can* invent something—but don't *have* to.

I presume that this is what lies behind the long-term plan of the ETs. What is the first question in religious instruction?

"Why are we on Earth?"

"We are on Earth to serve God and one day get to heaven."

In today's context the answer would be "We are on Earth to develop technologies and spread intelligence throughout the universe."

Why such complications? After all, the ETs already master the technologies and could spread them throughout space. They don't need humans for that.

Imagine that the ethnologists of a highly technological society visit a tribe of Stone Age humans. Are they supposed to instruct them how to build a car? Writing does not yet exist in the minds of the "stoneagers." Mathematics and all other arithmetical functions are unknown to them. The establishment of the first school would be just the starting shot for the development of society. There are neither steel works nor a battery factory for power. No sign of wheels, tires, compressed air, gearboxes, cogwheels, suspensions, brakes, filters, steering, spark plugs—let alone oils and fuel.

The ethnologists will not even attempt to teach the indigenous people how to build a car. The development into an industrialized state can only proceed in stages. That also applies to the universe. In space, millennia are not important. Imagine, further, that some intelligent species out there wants to know whether there are other intelligent beings within a distance of 800,000 light years. Do they broadcast radio signals on all imaginable frequencies? Get in touch! But radio signals are tied to the speed of light, which is about 300,000 kilometers per second. So do the astrophysicists of the intelligent species wait 1,600,000 years for a response? (800,000 years there and 800,000 years back.) And all of this purely in the hope that an answer might come trundling back. It might be, after all, that there is no other intelligence within a radius of 800,000 light years or one which does not want to respond.

There is no way around it. In order to exchange messages and experiences in the vast distances of the universe, an information network has to be built through time and space. This is underway. We are meant to be part of it. The development into an industrialized society took thousands of years. Great-great-great grandfathers found a way to mix metals into various alloys. Others tinkered around with plastics; others had great fun with lightning and thought up electricity. Off-road vehicles, tanks, aircraft, the atom bomb, and nuclear energy were developed. Industrialized nations arose, which today would certainly be in a position to construct giant spaceships. There are still knowledge gaps. Which rockets are the most effective? Does the "warp drive" from science-fiction films exist? How is speed faster than light possible? The curvature of space? Do "worm holes" exist? Could spaceships fly through them? Even if these impossible scenarios were possible, even if ETs jumped around the universe at a speed faster than light, this does not change anything in the development of the cosmic information network. Societies have to be built in space and time, which are capable of all these "impossible scenarios."

That is why we are being given help from outside. Thanks to their knowledge, we are already in a position to build smaller UFOs. What did Benjamin Robert Rich, the director of the secret Lockheed Skunk Works department, say? "We already have the possibility of flying to the stars...."[55] And the U.S. astronaut Ed Mitchell? "Not all UFOs are in fact extraterrestrial in origin. Some of them are our own development...but we are by no means at the technological level of those who visit us."[56] The ETs observing us neither want to kill us nor plunge the planet into panic. We are like them: created via chemical evolution to the Darwinian. As it is laid down in Holy Scripture, "And God said, Let us make man in our image, after our likeness...So God created man in his own image, in the image of God created he him; male and female created he them." (Genesis 1:26–27) Whereby only linguists know that the Hebrew word *Elohim*, used in the Bible for *God*, in truth is a plural term. *The gods.* Humanity has been watched over for thousands of years to the present day, including specific, artificial mutations of some leading figures. Even today—you haven't forgotten, have you?—some ETs live among us: "Some of the extraterrestrials look like us and could walk down the street without anyone noticing," proclaimed Theodor Hellyer, ex-defense minister of Canada.

"Actually quite a respectable model," says the opinion of one of my academic friends. "But that's all it is: a model. Everything dealt with here could also be explained differently without the intervention of ETs."

Correct. We humans can dissect everything. After all, it is a scientific maxim first to try the most obvious reasonable answer. And for that we do not need ETs. Yet the judgment as to *what* is the "most obvious possible" answer is a question of the zeitgeist.

Are UFOs a fact or not? Even with hundreds of thousands of erroneous reports, there remain a sufficient number of properly scientifically documented cases.

Are pictures really created in corn and other fields that were *not* made by fakers and grow within minutes?

Is there a group of a hundred scientists who legitimately show that neither chemical nor Darwinian evolution was possible without outside influence? Scientists who want nothing to do with "Creationism" or a belief in God?

Do we possess traditions that are thousands of years old and tell about humans and animals created by "the gods"? (Gilgamesh: Two-thirds god, one-third man. The Lamech Scroll with Noah's ancestry.)

There is more. Hundreds of cultures from antiquity to the time of the conquerors tell of the same independently of one another. All of them were visited by "gods," instructed by "gods," and there was artificial insemination.

This claim I intend to document in the next chapter.

CHAPTER 4

WHO WOULD HAVE THE SORRY COURAGE...

"Every myth, every legend reflects, as shown by science, a state or a real event.... And so to our great surprise, we find knowledge embedded in myths, albeit enciphered but not to be doubted, which early humans could not have acquired..."[1]

This quote comes from the ethnologist Karl Kohlenberg, who as long as 50 years ago was conducting comparative research into myths and reached the baffling conclusion: something is not quite right here. Why do Stone Age cultures that lived thousands of kilometers distant from one another and had no contact report related stories? Where do the conspicuous common elements originate? The very influential French classicist and ancient historian Professor Pierre Grimal (1912–1996) defined myth as "chronologically disordered history."[2] At their core, the original events had been preserved but frequently not in the correct causal context and, furthermore, in a wrong time.

Somewhere out there in indefinable space, "chaos" ruled. The world had not yet been created. Many of the oldest traditions start with this idea. Our ancestors could not imagine the origin of the universe. Are we better informed today? Someone created order in this chaos. Who? Where does this someone come from? The Greek poet Homer has Gaia arise and she in turn gives birth to Uranus—the starry heavens.[3] The Old Testament places chaos at the beginning. Then God enters stage right and creates order. He creates light, then water, land, vegetation, then the creatures of the sea, birds, and finally "cattle, and creeping things, and beasts of the earth" (Genesis 1:24), and on the sixth day, as the crowning glory of Creation, the human being.

How, actually, did the scribes of thousands of years ago know about the obligatory course of biological evolution? Human beings were not simply placed there as finished creatures. *Before* them there had to live other creatures, *before them* in turn sea creatures. That was only possible if land and water were first separated and an energy source—the sun—shone in the sky. The sequence is correct.

In Greek mythology, things are more confusing. The starry heavens—Uranus—produce the 12 Titans, male and female giants with immense strength. Their names are Oceanus, Coeus, Crius, Hyperion, Iapetus, Cronus, Theia, Rhea, Themis, Mnemosyne, Phoebe, und Tethys. They begat children and those in turn children. Thus were created Helios, the Sun god, and Selene, the Moon goddess. Cronus begat Poseidon and Zeus. There was war in the universe and on

Earth. Zeus fought against the dragon-like monster Typhon. Zeus finished the beast off with a lightning bolt. How else?

This Zeus (Latin for "Jupiter") is described by Homer as the father of all gods and humans. He gives earthly kings their power. Zeus is also the designer of a robot called Talos. This Talos circled the island of Crete several times a day and shot down anything that had no business on the island.[4] Zeus is also the father of Apollo, and he, in turn, is the teacher of young humanity. Apollo's main place of residence on Earth was Delphi, the location of the schools of wisdom and the Oracle. Delphi lies at the center of an incredible geometrical network that already existed in antiquity and was set up by gods of some kind.[5] Apollo, of course, possessed a heavenly chariot. He used it to fly each year to the "Land of the Hyperboreans which lay behind the north wind," but also over the ship Argo with its crew the "Argonauts."[6]

All human fantasy? Fire-breathing dragons? Fights in space? Flying machines? Robots?

Another of Zeus's sons was called Ares (Latin for "Mars"). He was a war-like being who was always in the company of Phobos and Deimos (fear and terror). Phobos and Deimos are still the current names of the two moons of Mars with their impossible orbits. They are definitely the strangest moons in our solar system. They orbit Mars in almost circular trajectories over the equator and they do so faster than Mars below them is rotating. Our astronomers say the two bodies are fragments from space that were once captured by Mars. This view has some snags. Both moons of Mars rotate in almost the same plane over the equator of Mars. *One* fragment might do that by chance, *two* is stretching things. In our time, several satellites have approached the moons of Mars and provided some quite good pictures. They are potato-like fragments with various craters from strikes. At a distance of 165 miles, the Mars Reconnaissance Orbiter also photographed a strange, monolith-like object with a clear, rectangular shadow. Buzz Aldrin, the second man on the moon, said, "There's a monolith there, a very unusual structure on this little potato-shaped object that goes around Mars once every seven hours." Next to the craters, parallel stripes have also been photographed on the surface. That is why the attempt was made to fly past Phobos and Deimos at a lower level. But no satellite from Earth reached its target. Our earthly probes went "blind" before they could transmit their images to Earth. Now we have two "potatoes with craters" but we know as little about the inner life of these small celestial bodies as we do about their orbit. In the autumn of 1972, the then-most famous Soviet astronomer, Iosif Shklovsky, at the Sternberg Institute in Moscow, told me, "I suspect that the two moons of Mars are hollow. Their orbits are not natural." Furthermore, the craters raise additional questions. It is generally known that debris from space strikes planets that do not have a protective atmosphere in which at least the smaller lumps would burn up. But why on such midgets like Phobos and Deimos? God knows the two don't possess the gravity of planets or larger moons. It is difficult to avoid the impression that at one time an incredible barrage of rocks flew through our solar system. From where? What was the cause? Star wars like the one fought by Zeus (and others!)? And was Ares, the son of Zeus, who created the Martian moons Phobos and Deimos, not a god of war?

Aphrodite (Latin for "Venus") and Hermes (Latin for "Mercury") were children of Zeus. People ascribed fantastical stories to them, yet the origin of all these myths remains shrouded in obscurity. The root of the Greek word *myein* (myth) contains the meaning of "mysterious." What Homer wrote about the gods was, in his time, already the result of a very long development. The gods were superhuman in the eyes of people, and yet they were similar to human beings. They lived in a kind of non-earthly state. They did not eat human food but ambrosia, the heavenly food, and drank nectar, the heavenly drink.

> The gods were imagined to be omniscient and omnipotent and yet there are things they don't know about what is happening in their immediate surroundings. They were also similar to humans in their form, just more beautiful and of more noble appearance.... They either reveal themselves to humans in their true shape or they transform themselves into human beings....[7]

So far the gods possess exceptional characteristics:

- They come from space.

- They are superhuman but of human form.

- They are technically far advanced of us: flying machines, robots, lightning weapons, Martian moons.

- They do not eat terrestrial food.

- Their shape is more beautiful than ours. They can transform themselves.

And where do humans come from? In almost all the traditions, they were created by heavenly beings. Greek myth reports that Prometheus, a son of the Titan Iapetus, had descended from heaven to Earth. The word *Prometheus* means "forethinker." This Prometheus possessed the knowledge of the gods and he also knew how the seed of heaven could be transplanted to Earth. So he took clay on Earth, wet it, and created a form out of it in the image of the gods."[8] Prometheus took the good characteristics of the animals and enclosed them in the human breast.

Animal characteristics are said to have been transferred to humans? Does there not resonate a primordial memory of an artificial mutation? Changes to the base sequence in the DNA molecule?

The first humans, so Greek mythology tells us, did not understand anything about their surroundings. They walked about like phantoms; they knew neither art nor technology. "Then Prometheus attended to these creatures: he taught them to observe the rising and setting of the celestial bodies, invented the art of counting for them, writing...but also shipbuilding...and taught human beings with regard to all other circumstances of life..."[9] Prometheus also instructed human beings in astronomy, metallurgy, and all kinds of sciences.

Other authors, some of them unknown, reported the same about that incomprehensible period. Diodorus of Sicily (Diodorus Siculus), for example, the historian from the first century before Christ, traveled the world for 30 years and visited all the libraries of antiquity. His historical work comprises 40 volumes. In the second volume, he writes that the first humans had literally learned everything from the gods, be it astronomy, metallurgy, road or house building, the art of writing, the healing arts, and whatever else. All of this must have happened in a very early time because it was the gods who taught human beings "not to eat one another."[10] When were our ancestors still cannibals?

Prometheus is also the one who brought fire to human beings. To do so he took a long stalk of giant fennel, held it against the passing chariot of the Sun, and in this way set the fennel alight. And soon the first fires were burning brightly on Earth. The supreme god, Zeus, saw this as treachery. He had poor Prometheus chained to a cliff of Mount Caucasus. In Christian/Jewish mythology, Lucifer starts a fight "in heaven" and resists the command of God with his armies. Lucifer is cast out of heaven and brings fire to Earth. "Lux fare" is Latin for "making fire."

Are all of them just silly stories? Myths? A hundred and forty years ago, the highly respected philologist Professor A. Wollheim, who had studied the ancient traditions that had been handed down, wrote, "Anyone who sees myths as just nonsensical tales and nice allegories has no idea of their importance. The myth is something quite different: *it is the most sublime expression of the most sublime truths. Furthermore, it is also the primordial history of humanity.*[11] (Author's italics)

Polynesia lies a long, long way from Greece. We understand it to mean the approximately 50 million square kilometers of Oceania from Hawaii in the north to New Zealand in the southwest, and Easter Island in the southeast. All of it is Polynesia—dreamily called the "South Seas" in popular parlance. This island world is awash with ancient traditions which —how could it be any other way—basically communicate the same content as in Greece. The creation story of the Maori in New Zealand tells about the creator god: "Io breathed in infinite space. The universe was in darkness. There was no glimmer from 'below,' of clarity, of light..."[12]

Like everywhere else, Io began to make light, create water and earth, then animals, and finally the first pair of humans. They were images of the cosmological primeval gods, created in their image. The inhabitants of the Marquesas Islands do not know anything different. They lie south of the equator, 1,600 kilometers northeast of Tahiti. (Politically, the Marquesas Islands belong to French Polynesia.)

"In the beginning the cosmos was in high heaven. Tanaoa lived in heaven...there was no voice, there was no music. Nothing living moved. There was no day, there was no night. There was only blackness, black darkness..."[13]

On the island of Samoa, the primeval god, who of course came from the cosmos, was called Tagaloa. Like everywhere else in Polynesia, the emptiness of the universe is first described. There is only 'chaos,' no light, no earth, no land, no sea, nothing on which something could grow. He had come from the infinitude of space, the great 'Tagaloa.' He had set lights over the earth, one for the day, another for the night. He had created land and water. Then he sowed the seed and created fish as well as animals on land. There are, so the tradition of the native inhabitants of Samoa says, nine different heavens and all of them are inhabited. Tagaloa appointed rulers over the different heavens, but also messengers between the heavens:

> Then Tagaloa, the creator, spoke to Tagaloa-le-fuli, "come here, I appoint you chief of the heavens." Then Tagaloa, the creator, spoke to Tagalos-savali, the messenger: "Come here, you shall be messenger between all the heavens. Starting with the eighth heaven to the first heaven. They shall all gather in the ninth heaven where Tagaloa-le-fuli rules."[14]

We learn that many stars are inhabited, but that is also what it says in many other original traditions. (I will come back to that.)

In the creation story of Hawaii, there are even three creator gods: Kane, Ku, and Lono. Each has different characteristics, but without exception they all came from space.

> And the wandering stars and the inhospitable stars, and the wandering stars of Kane, innumerable are the stars, the large stars, the small stars, the red stars of Kane. Oh infinite cosmos. The large moon of Kane, the large sun of Kane,

turning, moving in the immensity of the cosmos...and they created the human being in the image of Kane.[15]

Not one of these myths reached Polynesia through the white conquerors. It was not the Christian priests who taught the native inhabitants their knowledge. All traditions existed *before*. Jesus or other figures of Christian belief do not exist in the wide space of the Polynesian creation myth. Neither do any figures from the Old Testament such as Abraham or Moses. The ancient stories were told for x generations before there was contact with whites. And everywhere the stories begin with the endless cosmos. A god or some gods move in the blackness of the universe. There was neither above nor below, neither light nor shadow. The gods spent a very long time in this blackness until they were finally touched by the light of a sun. The path of the gods to Earth is described in more detail in the traditions of Kiribati. Kiribati is the collective name for a group of islands that stretch north and south of the equator. The islands belong both to Micronesia and Polynesia. Thirty-five years ago, I spent several days in the astonishingly well stocked library of "Bairiki," a village on the main island of Kiribati. There I studied the legends literally on site.

At the beginning, a long, long time ago, there was the god Nareau. No one knows from whence he came, who his parents were, *because Nareau flew alone and sleeping through space*. In sleep, he heard his name being called three times, but the caller was "nobody." Nareau awoke and looked around.

There was nothing but emptiness, but when he looked down he saw a large object. It was Te Bomatemaki—meaning "Earth and Sky together." Nareau's curiosity led him to descend and carefully set foot on Te Bomatemaki. There were no living creatures there, no animals, no humans. Just him, the creator. Four times he circumnavigated the world he had found from north to south, east to west, and he was alone. Finally Nareau dug a hole in Te Bomatemaki, filled it with water and sand, mixed both into rock and ordered the rock to give birth to Nareau Tekikiteia. Thus on instruction of the Creator, Nareau Tekikiteia was created, meaning "Nareau the Wise."

Nareau the Creator now ruled over Te-Bomatemaki, while Nareau the Wise was in the earth. Then Nareau the Wise created the first beings endowed with reason.

"And when the work was done, Nareau the Creator said, 'Enough! It is done! I go never to return!' And no one knows where he has been since then."[16, 17]

This ancient body of thought can be reasonably reinterpreted from today's perspective. Someone is flying alone and sleeping through space until he is woken by a voice who was "nobody." An astronaut lies in deep sleep. An on-board monitoring system registers a solar system with planets. The astronaut is woken by the computer, a "nobody." Below him, namely where there is the gravity of a celestial body, he notices a large object. The Earth. Once again in full command of his faculties, the pilot decides to land on the alien planet. ("Nareau stretched his limbs, he wanted to know what kind

of object it was...he descended and carefully set foot on it.")
Next the astronaut flies around the new planet from east to
west and from north to south. He finds no sign of life and
decides to plant the seeds of life. ("At that time there were
not yet any spirits nor any human beings but only mighty
Nareau. He went four times around the world...and determined that there was no life.")

The myth cannot tell by what means Nareau made life
flourish. Perhaps the processes were too confusing to be understood. ("Nareau dug a hole in the earth and filled it with
sand and water. Mixed both into rock...commanded the
earth to give birth. Thus Nareau the Wise was created.")

The characterization "the Wise" could stand for "spirit," "being ensouled," or "living." Where previously there
was emptiness life now begins to sprout. Now two elements
of creation are at work: Nareau the Creator of all existence
and Nareau the Wise for the start of terrestrial development.
("Nareau the Creator was now above Te-Bomatemaki, while
Nareau the Wise was in the earth.")

I have noticed a small difference between the principal god of Kiribati and the other super goods. Nareau
went, "never to return." Other divinities—Osiris (Egypt),
Quetzalcoatl (Mexico), Gesar (Tibet), Nommo (Mali), and
so on—expressly promised to return.

One island chain in the South Pacific is the New
Hebrides. The native inhabitants of Malekula (one of the islands) tell that a long time ago, Barakulkul had come from
heaven with five of his brothers. They did so in a coconut

which opened by itself.[18] This accords with the story from the Fiji Islands, for there the first humans emerged from a shiny egg which the cloud serpent "Degei" had thrown to earth.[19] For the Micronesians, heaven and earth were connected by ropes a long time ago. On one occasion, the brothers Tawaki and Karihi wanted to visit heaven. So they went to the place where the ropes were hanging down from heaven. One of the brothers managed by this means to reach the heavenly realms. And one of the Hawaiian gods, Lono by name, left Earth in a cloud ship. He did so with the express promise to return in the far distant future. The same applies to the youths Punifanga and Tafalin, both from Samoa, who "were borne up in the smoke of a might fire."[20] This immediately reminds us of Quetzalcoatl/Kukulkan, the feathered serpent of Central America. Be it the Maya, the Aztecs, or still earlier the Olmecs, all of them were familiar with the feathered/winged serpent that came from heaven and from which the original teachers emerged.

Professor Johannes Andersen, probably the foremost authority on all myths of Polynesia, author of a 500-page work on them, notes, "There are innumerable cosmological variants on the origin of the ancestral parents.... The expanses of space are mentioned multiple times and the infinitude of the universe."[21]

Not actually a surprise, one might think, for the South Sea Islands are tiny specks in the expanses of the Pacific Ocean. The native peoples stared upward each night, observed the course of the stars, and were lost in their reveries. But why did they think up the same or, at least, similar creation stories to the people in Egypt, Sumer, America, Australia, or China?

Psychologists such as C.G. Jung developed the idea of a common archetypal consciousness. Even if such an archetypal consciousness existed, where did it start? After all, even this archetypal consciousness had to start in a brain. Through which inspiration, influences, experiences?

I keep having to point out in my lectures and books that these archetypal memories *cannot* be events from nature. Why not? Stone Age people experienced natural disasters of all kinds: earthquakes, eclipses of the sun, volcanic eruptions, thunder, and lightning. They gave rise to the first nature religions. But the gods who came from the stars are not comparable because they supplied *information*. They acted as teachers. They instructed human beings in many fields of the sciences and technology. This is told by all historians of antiquity. No force of nature takes humans "up to heaven"—into the spaceship—and instructs them as follows: "Son of human beings, look outside. Do you see that small light out there? You humans call it the moon, but the moon does not have light of its own. It draws its light from the sun."[22] Then the person is told about the phases of the moon and about the course of the stars and the Earth around the sun, including leap hours. It can be read up in the Book of Enoch, chapters 72–75 and so on. And all this happened in the Stone Age because Enoch was the seventh patriarch before the Flood.

No nature religion will help us further, no lightning, no thunderstorm, and no earthquake. Scientific facts were communicated.

Often variants of the same myths were handed down by the same peoples, which should not come as a surprise. These traditions were handed down *before* there was writing. Stories were probably told through an endless relay from tribe to tribe, family to family, until it finally became possible to set them down in writing. The core nevertheless remained the same.

One of the Samoan legends tells about the god Tagaloa: "God Tagaloa lived in the universe. He created everything. He was alone, there was no heaven and no land. There was no water, no rock, neither sea nor earth. His original name was 'Tagaloa-fa-atuputupu-nu-u', which means 'Origin of Growth.'"[23]

As elsewhere, this primordial god creates the sun, then land, water, fishes, land animals and, as the pinnacle, human beings in the right sequence. This is described in the following way:

> Then Tagaloa spoke to the rock, and "Lua`o," a boy, came out. Then Tagaloa spoke again to the rock, and "Luavai," a girl, stepped out. Tagaloa brought both of them together...then Tagaloa made the spirit, the heart, the will, and the thinking.... Then said Tagaloa, may the spirit, the heart [feelings?], the will, and the thinking come

together in human beings. And they combined
and human beings were intelligent.[24]

The gods were always involved in the creation of human
beings. Yet as far as I am aware, not a single one of the creation myths reports that human beings had descended from
the apes or that some heavenly being had formed the human
being out of the chimpanzee. Oh yes—there is often talk of
liaisons between gods and humans, but not between humans
and apes.

Often the people of Polynesia linked their ancient stories with specific geographical locations. Thus the ancient
temple of Te-Mahara on the island of Raivavae (French
Polynesia) is today still deemed to be the location where the
god "Maui" landed after his space flight.[25] The native inhabitants of Ati Ona, one of the islands of the Marquesas group,
say the same. The small mountain Kei Ani is considered to
be a sacred place although there is no structure there. The
mountain was originally called Mouna-tuatini-etua, which
literally means "Mountain on which the gods landed."[26] And
of course (why should it be any different!) the South Sea is-
landers erected temples in honor of their heavenly teachers.
These rectangular structures are called *marae* and they can
be seen on many Polynesian islands.

The Marae Tooarai on Tahiti is a regular nine-stepped
pyramid, the one in Raiatea (French Polynesia) a rectangle made of monoliths. And even on the small island of
Borabora, which has a circumference of merely 14 kilometers, there are several, although smaller *maraea*. Nowhere
did I find sculptures chiseled into the stone. No depiction

The Marae of Arahurahu on Tahiti consists of several terraces.
Photo credit: Erich von Daniken, Beatenberg/Schweiz

The Marae of Raiatea in French Polynesia, a former landing site of the
gods. Photo credit: Erich von Daniken, Beatenberg/Schweiz

of the gods, such as, for example, on the Maya pyramids in Mexico. Just simple terraces or platforms in memory of and as waiting rooms for the gods.

Reinhard Habeck, a thoroughly honest researcher and author of many books on the subject of extraterrestrials refers to a "cowshed of god" in an article for the magazine *Ancient Skies* (currently *Sagenhafte Zeiten*).[27] This is a circular wooden building constructed by a Dinka tribe in Upper Sudan. Despite having a large diameter of 12 meters, the round house is empty. It serves as a sacred site in honor of a god called Mayual, who is said to have ascended to heaven from this site.

Many peoples honored their gods in places that later became sacred sites. This is what happened to a majority of the gigantic temples of antiquity. They arose everywhere where the gods were once active. The oldest Maya city of Tikal is located in what is Guatemala today. But it was only founded because the "ruler of the heavenly family" had once descended here. This is what is inscribed on a small Mayan plate, the so-called "Leyden Plate," which is today kept in the Museum of Leyden in the Netherlands. Another of these ancient locations, 20 kilometers east of the Euphrates (south of Baghdad, Iraq) was called Uruk. (Biblical Erech, Greek Orchoi, Roman Orchoe.) Today it is Warka. Uruk existed as long ago as the fourth century before Christ and is the location where the oldest writings were found, including the Sumerian text "Bilgamesh and Akka." (Not **G**ilgamesh.) The cuneiform script tells about a temple built in honor of "An, who has descended from heaven." The structure was erected "where a cloud spread over the earth...where a start was made from earth...where the magnificence of An started from the earth...."[28]

The god Enlil and the heavenly goddess Inana originally resided in Uruk. They maintained "the bond between heaven and earth."[29] The geographical space in which the incomprehensible occurred is a glob on the globe. Mesopotamia, the home territory of the earlier Chaldeans, the Sumerians, and the Babylonians, is only an hour by plane from Egypt. That is why a brief link with my book *Evidence of the Gods* is appropriate here:

> In the Pyramid Texts of Unas from the Third Dynasty, researchers keep encountering verses (so-called "Utterances") in which the Pharaoh literally flies in a heavenly barque:
>
> (Utt. 267) "A stairway to heaven has been set up for me so that I can ascend to heaven... and I climbed up on the smoke of the large vessel. I fly high as a bird and light as a beetle on the empty throne of your barque, oh Re. And I am permitted to sit on your seat and thunder across heaven, oh Re. I am permitted to lift off the land in your barque..."
>
> (Utt. 434) "You have helped every god who possesses an own barque so that they set themselves up in the starry heavens..."

(Utt. 584): "The doors of the (?)...which are in the firmament were opened for me, the metal doors which are in starry heaven lie open for me..."[30]

There are many of these verses but our confused zeitgeist turns them into wishful thinking. The priests had imagined journeys of the pharaohs after death. This is nothing but scientifically misunderstood nonsense. Our busy Egyptologists are not aware of the links with ancient India. There, too, the leaders of humanity are ferried about in flying vehicles, so-called "vimanas." The following extracts are a few examples:

"'Faster Matali!' spoke Indra. 'Be quick with my heavenly chariot...' Matali steered the chariot which gleamed like a sunbeam to the place where Rama encountered his enemies. Take this heavenly chariot, Matali called out to Rama...dressed in heavenly materials, Rama mounted the chariot and threw himself into battle such as human eyes had never seen before...."[31]

"While Kalki is still speaking, two chariots descend from heaven, gleaming like the sun, made of gems of all kinds, moving by themselves, protected by incandescent weapons."[32]

"So the king sat down...in the heavenly chariot. They reached the expanse of the firmament.... The heavenly chariot flew around the earth over the oceans towards the city of Avantis where a festival was just being held.... After a short stopover, the king started again under the eyes of innumerable onlookers who marveled at the heavenly chariot."[33]

And these gods were never squeamish. The terrestrial rulers supplied the "heavenly" beings with gold and diamonds. In return, they were protected.

> Thereupon Hor-Hut flew up into the firmament in the form of a large sun disc with wings attached... when he saw the enemies from the heavenly heights, he charged upon them with such might that they neither saw nor heard him. Within a short period of time, no living head existed any longer. Hor-Hut, shining in many different colors, returned to the ship of Ra-Harmachis in his shape as a large, winged sun disc.[34]

There is no shortage of stories about flying vehicles in antiquity. The busy critics have no idea about this. King Solomon gave his lover, the Queen of Sheba, a flying chariot: "He gave her all the splendors she could wish for...and vehicles with which to drive on land, *and a chariot which flew through the air* which he had made in accordance with the wisdom given him by God."[35] (Author's italics) We even know about the speed of Solomon's flying chariot: "The king and all under his command, they flew on the wagon without sickness and suffering, without hunger and thirst, without sweat and exhaustion, *covering a distance of three months in one day.*"[36] (Author's italics)

These were facts recorded thousands of years ago. That our busy Egyptologists and Sumerologists turned this into legend is understandable. The zeitgeist was not yet ready for the logical consequences. But meanwhile the links can be shown; exegesis—the interpretation—is no longer isolated to a geographical region. Myths are *the most sublime expression of the most sublime truths and much more. They are the primordial history of humanity*," according to Professor A. Wollheim 140 years ago.[37]

If we accept as a factor in even just one example that gods equal extraterrestrials, all the creation myths abruptly make sense from Greece through Polynesia to the jealous God of the Old Testament. And this simple insight also throws a light on certain construction technologies in ancient history. Once accepted, illumination passes around the world.

Even the soil of Kiev, the capital of Ukraine, was the landing site of the god Perun thousands of years ago. Starokyivska Hill lies in the center of Kiev. Until the ninth century it had a religious building in honor of Perun, who long ago "descended from heaven in a pillar of fire" in precisely this place.[38] Like Zeus in Greece or Odin in Germania, Perun was deemed to be the "god of lightning" who drove around the earth in his heavenly chariot. Originally the sacred site for this flying god comprised an area of 10,000 m^2. This has been shown by archeological investigations in Kiev.[39] Most of these ancient sacred sites were destroyed with the advent of Christianity. This happened (almost) worldwide.

We are quite well informed about the heavenly beings who came from the cosmos in silver and golden eggs in the pre-Inca period. Both in South and Central America, priests traveled to the newly discovered lands soon after the first conquerors. Their job was to bring Christianity to the native peoples. But the bearded and not very pleasantly smelling ecclesiastics also noted what the indigenous inhabitants were telling them about their gods, written down more than four centuries ago when flying was not yet occupying our minds. There were reports about "golden and silver eggs out of which came the teachers, the heavenly nobles."[40,41]

The Spanish chronicler Pedro Simon writes that a priest from the Chibcha tribe had told him the following about the beginning of all things: "It was night. There was still something of the world. The light was locked up in a large 'something hut' and emerged from it. This 'something hut' is Chiminigagua and it contained the light within itself so that it would come out. Then things began to be."[42]

The Chibcha are a tribe in the highlands and the valleys of the eastern Colombian cordillera. Logically they had no understanding of extraterrestrial technology. So the spaceship became a "something hut." No different than distant Easter Island. The primordial gods were venerated as "masters of the universe." They include Makemake, the inhabitant of the air. His symbol is the egg.[43] And the same thing exists thousands of kilometers away in the highlands of Tibet. The so-called "Books of Kandshur and Tandshur" tell clearly about "pearls in the heavens" as well as of "shining glass spheres" from which the gods emerged.[44] "Kandshur and Tandshur" are not actual books but folios in which the sacred texts of Lamaism are recorded. The term *Tandshur* means "translated teaching" and is a commentary on the "Kandshur." No one knows their original age.

The similarities in the content of sacred books is always intriguing although their authors could not know anything about one another. So the Inuit say that their great-, great-, grandfathers once came to present-day Alaska in "flying houses."[45] And the Tungus, a tribe in Siberia, claim their first divine couple had descended from heaven "in a silver gondola." That is precisely how it was recorded by the famous polar explorer Fridtjof Nansen in his book *The First Crossing of Greenland*.[46] The work was published in 1891, once again a time when aircraft were unknown.

It is the same across the world. In ancient Egypt, Nun was seen as the endless ocean of stars from which the primal god Osiris had once arrived in a "golden ship."[47] Just like the gods, his spouse Isis descended in a silver barque from Sirius to human beings. Osiris and Isis, the heavenly couple from Orion and Sirius. It was no different in Nippur, the millennia-old Sumerian city. The place is called Nuffar today and lies about 180 kilometers southeast of Baghdad. It once had step pyramids in honor of Enlil and Ninlil. Like in Uruk, tablets made of lapis lazuli (lapis is a blue shiny mineral) were also found in Nippur, which praised the two gods "because they maintain the bond between heaven and earth."[48] Why, then, is there something similar in the

Finnish national epic *Kalevala*? God knows the far north has nothing to do with Baghdad in the south. The Finns refer to a "flame bird," which brought wisdom from heaven and was also involved in fighting in the firmament.[49]

We can leap around the globe. Cultures that have never met, never heard of one another, report about similar events which, without exception, took place in a dark age when there was not yet any writing. Just being surprised about that is not enough. We have to draw the conclusions. Human beings experienced the arrival of their primal gods from the cosmos. Once there was writing, their memories migrated to clay tablets, palm leaves, and wooden boards. Later they turned into stone sculptures. The experiences of the venerable ancestors were to remain unforgotten forever. Thus, they grew to become an element of the cultural heritage, the religions, and were celebrated in folk dances or priestly song. The powerful impact of the past, the mystery of the heavenly teachers, was never to fade from memory. After all, those gods had promised to return one day. Nothing surprises me any longer. The gods were visitors from alien solar systems. What else? In Exodus the descent of God is described in the following words: "And Mount Sinai was altogether on a smoke, because the Lord descended upon it in fire: and the smoke thereof ascended as the smoke of a furnace, and the whole mount quaked greatly." (Exodus 19:18)

What did we turn that into? Religion. Those who don't want to know go on about how it was only a tropical storm or volcanic eruption—and ignore that the tropical storm or volcanic eruption gave precise instructions. There was a flow of information. God has spoken. The faithful, in turn, see the true and only God behind it. As if the being of God, the sublime figure of Creation, would care about a small ethnic group on a ridiculous world called Earth among trillions of planets. Even more insane, as if he would go racing about on this insignificant planet with a vehicle that descends on a mountain in "smoke and fire" and makes it glow. Whereby the same "God" still issued the instruction *before* his landing to erect a fence around the mountain to avoid the people being harmed. All previous attempts at an explanation, no matter how clever and profound the intention, are on a hiding to nothing. The facts should determine our insight—not religious or psychological wishful thinking.

What facts? Those of the temples across the world in honor of the gods. Teotihuacan in Mexico, the place "at which the gods conferred," the place also "at which the gods are buried."[50] "During the period of night, when the sun did not yet shine, when there was not yet day, the gods assembled at the place called Teotihuacan."[51] And this Teotihuacan is not some one-horse town where a few temples are located. All the buildings on the main street, the "Avenida de los muertes," form a model of our solar system, including Uranus, Neptune, and Pluto about which the Stone Age planners could not know anything—other than through the gods, the teachers.[52] Uruk, one of five cities in Mesopotamia founded by the gods, was modeled on a heavenly city on another star.[53] "In China, Hangzhou, Marco Polo's Ling-gan or King-se, was called the 'heavenly city.' They believed their city was an image of the cities of the gods in the heavens," writes the ethnologist Karl F. Kohlenberg.[54] And in Beijing, in the middle of the capital of the Chinese empire, there stands the Palace of Heavenly Emperors. Just like that? So that atheistic China remembers a "heavenly emperor"?

How divorced from the world does theology and comparative religion have to be to avoid bringing the facts in the ancient texts, the sculptures, the rituals, and the "heavenly cities" under one umbrella? An umbrella, by the way, which covers a multitude of things and provides a meaningful explanation for everything.

Rome, the Holy City. Why is it located where it is? The god of war, Mars, once made a king's daughter pregnant. What else? She gave birth to twins, Romulus and Remus. The children were set adrift on the river Tiber in a willow basket (remember Moses in the basket on the Nile) and were ultimately nursed by a female wolf. Decades later, Romulus had long become king, and the god Jupiter kidnapped Romulus and took him to heaven. From that time on, his divine name was "Quirinus." And the location of these incomprehensible events was called Rome.[55]

Among the Germanic peoples, the supreme god was called Odin (also Wotan, the angry one). Of course his parents Bos and Bestla came from heaven. In the land of the gods, in Asgard, he sat on a throne and could oversee both the world of the gods and the world of humans. His war horse had eight legs and was the fastest means of transport in the firmament. On his shoulders sat the holy ravens Huginn and

Muninn, who on their wings could see everything that was happening on Earth. What was that in Egypt? Nothing on Earth escaped the falcon Horus, a son of Osiris and Isis. The eye of Horus is keeping watch.

Thor (Donar the thunderer) was a son of Odin and—as so often—a mixture between heaven and earth. Thor's mother was accordingly the human Jord. Thor's tool was a gigantic hammer that hung on a magic belt. The innumerable enemies that Thor slaughtered also included the architect Thyrm. Why did Thor kill Thyrm? Because the latter was meant to build the fortress of the gods Asgard, but something went wrong. In the end, many descendants of the gods landed in Valhalla.[56] And this, in turn, is not located in some arbitrary spot on Earth. Take a map of Germany and draw a line through the present-day cities of Aachen, Frankfurt, Würzburg, Nuremberg, and Donaustauf. All these points have their origin in the Stone Age and can be connected with a dead straight line. After about 300 kilometers as the crow flies, the stretch ends at a hill behind Donaustauf. That is where the temple complex of Valhalla is located.

Nowadays tourists drive up to the impressive columned hall by car. The temple in honor of great Germans was built by King Ludwig I of Bavaria (1786–1868), but according to legend, the original Valhalla, the funerary temple of the god Odin, was in the region.

Communities, cultures, and peoples are all connected by myth. In the view of the East African Massai, who are located mostly in the south of Kenya, there once lived upon earth a

Valhalla near Donaustauf in Bavaria, Germany.
Photo credit: Tourismus Donaustauf/Deutschland

young man by the name of Kintu and he fell in love with the daughter of a heavenly being that had visited Earth. The father permitted Kintu to go to heaven for a time to learn. But when the pair remained in love also in the heavenly realms, the father sent both of them back to Earth to instruct humans in all matters.[57] This is very similar to the myth of the Bantu peoples in today's South Africa. There the heavenly god Nzame had descended to Earth to investigate the planet. Here he fell in love with the extremely beautiful human woman Mboja. The pair begat a son and called him Bingo. The supreme god was angry about this cross between a celestial and terrestrial being and the two of them were not allowed to return to heaven. The pair instructed humans in all matters and now we know the origin of the popular expression "Bingo." Bingo! The Shilluk tribes in southern Sudan say that the first human being, Omara, had originally come from heaven. At that time, humans still lived like wild animals and killed one another. But Omara weaned them away from the animals and taught them everything they needed to know. Omara had also founded the first kingdom on Earth.[58]

Always the same: The original teachers always came from the stars. The Nuba tribe lives primarily in the middle of Sudan and forms the largest non-Arab group. They are a group of more than a million people, which nevertheless speak different languages. All of them have the creation myth in common according to which the heavenly god Nuba ordered his divine messenger Su to bring grain to humans. To this end, he was to lower the grain kernels "from heaven to earth on a long bamboo pole. As soon as the kernels had arrived on earth, the messenger of the gods was to beat a drum."[59] (According to other versions, he lowers it on a long hemp rope.) As soon as the heavenly god heard the sound of the drum, he intended to pull the bamboo pole up again so that humans could not use it to climb up to heaven. But the divine messenger was driven by curiosity and he opened the sack of grain before he reached Earth. Now some of the kernels fell down directly on to the drum. The heavenly god heard the faint drum beats and thought his messenger had reached Earth. So he quickly pulled the bamboo pole up again. The messenger fell to Earth and with him the sack full of grain, which broke open on the ground. So the divine messenger showed humans the grain and taught them how to make fields and grow cereals.

Here the question arises as to the origin of certain foods. Both the Central and South American tribes hold the view that maize was brought to Earth by the gods and originally in four colors: yellow, white, red, and black. The same applies to bananas. There is no knowledge of an "original banana." Rice too is supposed to be a gift from heaven, the brilliant Indologist Armin Risi reports.[60]

I wrote extensively about the Dogon tribe in the Republic of Mali, in my last book.[61] Their heavenly teacher was called Nomo and came from the constellation of Sirius. This Nomo also told the Dogon about the Sirius system. He explained to them that Sirius was a dual star (currently Sirius A + B) and that there were still additional celestial bodies in the system (which are still unknown to our astronomers).

South American peoples, including the Inca and Warao tribes, even say that originally humans had lived in heaven and had descended from time to time to hunt here. It was only later that they settled here. But they had sporadically been visited again and taught by their heavenly ancestors. Reports of the same kind can be found among the Kogi Indians in Colombia. They live in the mountains on the Caribbean side of Colombia. Their original heavenly teachers created the first humans, instructed them in all matters, and continue to visit them even today. It was the same teachers who warned human beings thousands of years ago about a flood which would be intentionally caused and ordered them to build ships. "And the priests, the older brothers, all descended from heaven...."[62,63]

That is astonishing for a lateral thinker like myself, for the same story was told worlds and oceans away from Colombia. The Sumerian King List <WB444>, currently in the British Museum in London, says, "After the flood had passed, the kingdom descended from heaven once more." And the same is told in the Gilgamesh epic, which also originates from Sumer. After the flood, the gods descended from the heavens.

Who would have the sorry courage to ignore this worldwide accumulation of statements? In *what* age are we living? In the 17th century or the age of global communications? The Tootoosh native peoples on the northwest coast of California not only report about a Thunderbird, which descended from the heavens and instructed their ancestors, but they also still represent this Thunderbird on their totem poles today. The Hopi in Arizona—this is something my loyal readers are familiar with—know about the heavenly teachers and naturally venerate these teachers in the form of dolls. "The first world was Tokpela, the endless universe. But right at the beginning, so our elders tell us, there was only the creator Taiowa. Around him was infinite space. There was neither a beginning nor an end, neither time nor form. Just immeasurable emptiness...."[64] That is how it has been handed down in the *Book of the Hopi*, the collection of myths of this Native American tribe that today lives in Arizona. And White Bear, the oldest Hopi, described to the NASA designer Josef Blumrich what originally happened:

> This is the story of my ancestors and the clans
> who came to this part of the world. The continent
> on which my people lived for a long time sank
> into the sea and the people had to leave it.... In the
> first world the deity Taiowa created human be-
> ings.... He gave them reason, he gave them knowl-
> edge, he gave them all the things they need for
> their life. And he gave them the law and the du-
> ties they had to fulfill in this part of the world.[65]

And as a cross-connection for new readers: Naturally the Kayapo on the upper Amazon, 8,000 kilometers distant from the Hopi, know the same thing and celebrate it in their danc- es even today. These, then, are not just obscure tales hand- ed down but verifiable evidence: totem poles, kachina dolls, Kayapo dances, gods who have descended chiseled in stone worldwide, sacred places where the gods were once at work, and so on. We call all of this illustrative material. Bingo!

And how do we act? We continue to live in the dulled, sticky mess of the psychology of religion, which has answers to everything, none of which are true. Two years ago, I spoke at the theological faculty of a Swiss university in the depart- ment of comparative religions—a quite ordinary lecture in a quite ordinary lecture hall with 30 quite ordinary students. I spoke about flying vehicles in the ancient Indian writings, the so-called "vimanas." When I had finished, the dean of the faculty explained to his students how these texts were to be understood. "When a young man today drives through the landscape in his open top car, his hair flutters in the wind. He has the feeling that he is flying. That is what happened thousands of years ago. At that time the offspring of the prosperous rulers drove into the arena in richly decorated chariots, often with pearls, and drawn by four horses. Their long hair fluttered in the wind. They thought they were flying...."

And I thought I was dreaming. In the ancient Indian texts there is clear differentiation between chariots with wheels that roll on the ground, and those without wheels that fly over and above the Earth and even to the moon. But in the theological faculties, even those teaching comparative religion, people still live in the Middle Ages. Nothing new is added. The same applies with regard to the most sacred book of Christianity: the Bible. Theologians persist in proclaiming that the Bible contains the Word of God. The famous Jesuit and professor of theology, Karl Rahner, the mentor of whole hosts of young priests, asserts that the story of the Old Testament "came from *the* God who ultimately revealed himself in Jesus Christ." The scripture of the Old and New Testament had the same originator. The Old Testament was from the beginning "an open progression towards final salvation steered by God."[66] And the theology professor Jacques Guillet teaches that the stories in the Bible were "without exception reports about the fulfillment of a Word of God. This schema applies in all cases."[67] Aha! In fact, and every theologian should know this, the Old Testament is a work full of contradictions, written by innumerable authors at various times. And often texts from outside sources were inserted. (For example, the story of the Flood that comes from much older Sumerian writings, or the stirring story of the little boy Moses who floated down the Nile in a little basket. The same is already reported about the Babylonian ruler Sargon I, a thousand years before Moses.) The Old Testament glorifies a pseudo god who descends to humans in smoke, fire, noise, and heat. In this context even the vehicle of this "God" is described in detail in the book of Ezekiel. And since my first work, *Chariots of the Gods*, a copy of that "heavenly vehicle" has been drawn by a NASA rocket engineer.[68, 69] We *know* today what Ezekiel was describing. A similar thing applies to biblical manna or the Ark of the Covenant. Modern knowledge exposes the Ark of the Covenant as a life-threatening technical device which, furthermore, "is not of this earth."[70]

The explanations of our time are without exception sensible, logical, and scientifically comprehensible. But that is of no interest to any theologian. Professor Hermann Oberth (1894–1989), the "father of space travel," told me some years ago, "There are scholars who behave like stuffed geese. They no longer take in new knowledge."

The book of the Old Testament prophet Job describes a "leviathan" as follows (Chapter 40):

> His bones are as strong pieces of brass; his bones are like bars of iron...Out of his mouth go burning lamps, and sparks of fire leap out. Out of his nostrils goeth smoke, as out of a seething pot or caldron. His breath kindleth coals, and a flame goeth out of his mouth.... When he raiseth up himself, the mighty are afraid: by reason of

breakings, they purify themselves. The sword of him that layeth at him cannot hold: the spear, the dart, nor the habergeon.

What is being described here? Jacques Guillet says, "Without exception reports about the fulfillment of a Word of God. This schema applies in all cases."

There are in our time increasing numbers of books by authors who can read the "Book of Books" in various languages and who correctly analyze the nonsense that has been interpreted into the Old Testament. Thus Walter Jörg Langbein, theologian and comrade-in-arms from the beginning, picks apart "Holy Scripture" and uncovers the various original sources that were raided to make the Bible.[71] His analyses appear to have provoked as little interest as the work of Mauro Biglino, who fluently reads Hebrew and knows all the links to the Aramaic and Semitic roots.[72] In Mauro Biglino it becomes clear that angels were nothing other than extraterrestrials and that there is a crucial difference between angels and cherubim: "While angels are persons, cherubim are machines!"[73] Every Bible reader is left with the belief that a single great God has been at work in the Old Testament. Nothing of the kind is true. The reference is always to the "Elohim," the gods *in plural.* Accordingly the translation regarding the creation of the human being is not "And God said, Let us make man in our image, after our likeness," but "...we want to make man in our image..."[74]

A fairy tale? No. It is the concordant primal memory of human beings and the same is reflected in the tales worldwide.

"Long ago there was a time in which all people lived up in heaven..."[75] So starts one of the creation myths of the Inuit. "Moon spirits" and "heavenly beings" created the first humans and later there was also sexual contact between the "moon spirits" and Inuit women.

The Japanese tribe of the Yamasachi tells of a time "when there were still demigods on Earth who commuted between heaven and Earth as they wished."[76] Like elsewhere, here too it came to sexual intercourse between the "offspring of a heavenly deity" and humans. The product was—what else?— half gods, half humans. The Japanese Amewakahiko kings founded their ruling house directly together with heaven: "The origin of our ruling house extends back into the age of the gods. With Jimmu Tennô, the sequence of terrestrial rulers begins.... Now because this land is a land of the gods, it happens from time to time that gods live as humans among us and unite with humans..."[77] Something similar can be heard in the world of Egyptian tales. All rulers of the Old Kingdom descended directly from some god or other.[78] And those gods expressly wanted humans who were similar to them.

Kings as sons of the gods? Tibet, China, Greece, and many more say hello. Flying chariots in ancient India, with Solomon, in the Bible? Already heard the one about the flying carpets in the Arabian and Persian tales?[79] The knowledge of visits by gods and the creation of humans is global. Not to recognize this is thoroughly unscientific. And the psychological variations that keep being wheeled out in explanation of this fantastical reality are no more than grumpy vanity.

The Baltic Latvian people may be more closely related to us than remote King Solomon. Their principal god was called Dievs. (For the Romans, "gods" = "die." In French today, still "god" = "dieux.") Dievs lived in heaven and ruled there over vast riches. He rode around the heavenly mountain on his flying horse and, at the time of the terrestrial harvest, descended from heaven to earth.[80] Chinese mythology is familiar with nine heavens, whereby the supreme heavenly god resided in the constellation of the Great Bear.[81] The original emperors reached the earth with fire-breathing dragons. In the Tibetan highlands, it is not just the first ruler, Gesar, who came from space but also many other gods.[82] And how? "Heaven resounded, the earth shook, there was the roaring of dragons." The quote could come from the Old Testament. But it doesn't. It comes from Tibetan mythology. Other heavenly beings of Tibet "used a rope or ladder to descend.... Many sons of gods descend from the heaven of the gods to the earth of humans. They then become the rulers and kings of human beings."[83]

Tierra del Fuego, the southern tip of South America, is poles apart from Tibet. Like everywhere else, the primal human being, Kenos, came to Earth to bring order to it. "Then he flew back to heaven; he now lives among the stars."[84] It is no different among the Pawnee people in what is Nebraska today. According to their teaching, humans were created by stellar beings and the heavenly ones had come down to us repeatedly "with fire and smoke."[85] (Food for thought: There are 11,000 kilometers as the crow flies between Tierra del Fuego in South America and the great plains of the USA.)

We lack perspective. Every scientist, however hard working, has to specialize. There is no alternative. Knowledge has become too extensive. The paradox here? Specialization is precisely the reason *why* the connections fail to be seen. It is *impossible* for an Egyptologist to know the Indian writings of the *Mahabharata*. All the texts from the field of ancient India are not even known to the specialists in Indology. There are simply too many. If even the Indologists don't have a complete overview, how, then, is the Egyptologist supposed to learn about the gigantic body of Indian literature alongside his own specialism? Of course! Super computers could show the links—to the extent that the texts were previously scanned in and the right program existed. Personally I need six months to battle my way even superficially through the *Mahabharata* and specifically the "Drona Parva" (part of the *Mahabharata*).[86] Scholars who make this effort just once in their lives know for all eternity that the ancient gods can only be a reference to space travelers from distant worlds. Among those knowledgeable about the ancient Indian texts, any discussion about alien space travelers thousands of years ago only provokes a weary smile. Of course they were here. Anyone who still disputes this does not know the comprehensive textual material. The "Drona Parva" describes space ships in the firmament, then terrible "heavenly" weapons in comparison to which every tropical storm, every earthquake, every volcanic eruption is a mere hiccup. There was clear differentiation between "cities in the firmament"—we would describe them as "generational spaceships" today—and smaller space shuttles. Whereby, and this is worth noting, the men who translated these texts from Sanskrit into English lived in the last century, except one.[87] Therefore they couldn't have the faintest idea about mother spaceships, aircraft, space shuttles, etc. The translation of verse 50 in the "Drona Parva" says specifically, "The three cities came together in the firmament." It was translated in 1888![88] Weapons systems are described that burn everything through "concentrated heat rays," others are activated through the eyes of the pilot. Then there are hypnotic weapons or weapons that produce illusions in the firmament. Weapons that can make mountain chains explode and others that could tear open the whole planet if they were deployed. The "Drona Parva" describes aerial battles between different armed flying machines, which can change their position in the firmament at lightning speed. This is where we need a short quote from my book *Habe Ich Mich Geirrt?*

> Scorched by the heat of the weapons, the world staggered in heat. Elephants were burned and stumbled about...The water boiled, all the fishes died...The trees fell by the dozen...Horses and war chariots burned up...It was a nightmarish sight. The dead bodies were mutilated from the terrible heat; they no longer looked human. Never before

has there been such a gruesome weapon, never before have we heard of such a weapon....[89]

The hair of the warriors and their fingernails and toe-nails fell out from the effect of this weapon. All life paled because it was overlaid with the "deadly breath" of the god. And far from where the weapon was deployed, even the un-born children died in their mother's wombs.

We Westerners have no idea. We bask in the feeling of being the greatest, indeed, the pinnacle of evolution. We don't care about the ancient traditions of cultures. And the weapons systems in the thousand-year-old texts of the "Drona Parva" have long been adequately explained. They were "tropical storms."[90] Since when do tropical storms cause the effects described? And since when are tropical storms also responsible for deadly radiation that kills unborn children in their mother's wombs? And in any case, how did people thousands of years ago know anything at all about deadly radiation? We are resting on the completely false laurels of our self-aggrandizement. The flying chariots of thousands of years ago? Nothing but "meaningless chatter" and "foolish fantasies," so said Professor Hermann Jacobi 160 years ago.[91]

One hundred and sixty years in the past! Yet the views of yesteryear, at the time probably carefully considered by highly intelligent professors with great integrity, have at no time since then been questioned, at least not by the relevant scientists. There is no "new school." The old knowledge is gumming up the brains. And books like the present one or those of my outstanding colleagues don't count. Why? I said so in the Introduction: *Because its hypotheses and evidence do not fit into the laboriously constructed mosaic of established conventional wisdom, scholars will put it on the list of those utopian books which it is advisable not to talk about.*

What to do? Provide enlightenment and let the zeitgeist do its work.

The Bantu tribe in Cameroon tells of its oldest patriarch that he flew down to their tribal homeland in a large hollowed-out tree. "Everything we can see was made by Mubei. First he made the earth...then the grass steppes... then put the animals on them.... Nyoenduma made a great rock rain. Whereupon it opened with great thunder and brought forth the first two humans."[92]

Humans created by some "heavenly beings"? This is also told by the small tribe of the Abasi in West Africa. Abasi brought the people living in heaven directly to Earth. "He created all things. All things above, all things below. He created the water and the forest and the rivers and the springs and the animals. He created all the things that are there in the whole world, but he did not create the human beings...because they lived aloft with Abasi in his heavenly city."[93]

A "heavenly city" was also inhabited by the King of Salem, a priest of the supreme God of the Jews.[94] *Or* the Tibetan son of heaven, Gesar. He originally lived in a flying city that shone in the firmament and "possessed roofs of heavenly iron which resisted every lightning bolt."[95] *Or* the Arab historian Nashwan Ibn Said, who died around 1195, and who told about "a city of metal," which had in the past appeared out of nothingness. The whole town had stood on "silver, gleaming pillars" and water had been guided through the facilities in metal channels.[96] *Or* Hadhad, father of Bilqis (Queen of Sheba). His residence was "a flying palace made of metal and towers."[97] *Or*, as already mentioned, the "three cities in the firmament" in the ancient Indian "Drona Parva."[98] *Or* "cities in the heavens which gleamed like crystals," described in the Book of Enoch.[99] *Or...or...*there are many such examples. Heavenly cities are simply a part of the traditions of peoples. Be it the most forgotten tribe somewhere in Africa, be it in the highlands of Tibet, or be it in the profound books of the ancient Jews.

Humans had to be able to speak before they learned to write. The first language was dictated by the gods. That is what several historians of antiquity say.[100, 101, 102] "Human beings are only human through language; but in order to invent language they already had to be human."[103] The quote comes from the statesman and scholar Wilhelm von Humboldt (1787–1835). A bush is a bush and not a moon. The sun is an illuminated sphere in the firmament and not a water course. Human beings are human beings and neither crocodile nor bird. In order to understand one another, the first humans had to mean the same thing. Only then does writing become possible. Moses was given the tablets of the law—if we believe the Old Testament—from his "God" on Mount Sinai. The Sumerians were given writing by the god An.[104] It is no different in Tibet, India, or China. "We recall the fact that originally all letters and pictograms and characters were deemed without exception to be sacred by all peoples and were only comprehensible to the priests. According to that view, writing also came from the stars,"[105] as Karl Kohlenberg, with his thorough knowledge of myths, confirms. Then, in about 1,600 BC this Hammurabi (1728–1686) appears, who—how could it be otherwise—was born in heaven. His mother was made pregnant by the sun god. Naturally, Hammurabi became the King of Babylon and as such he left a splendid body of law: the Code of Hammurabi. The text had been chiseled into an over two-meter high stone pillar, which was excavated at the start of the 20th century in Susa, what today is Shush in Iraq. In his laws, Hammurabi explicitly refers to "divine revelation."[106] We should be able to assume that the legislator will not start his imposing work with a whopping lie. But a lot is possible among politicians. In 280 paragraphs, the people now know about the law, but also about the financial system, the rules of inheritance, or of marriage. The Code of Hammurabi deals with several categories of people. There were those who were free, semi-free, and slaves. But within this class system, all people were equal. The free people had to adhere to the rules between one another, as did the semi-free people and slaves. Some examples:

> If a man breaks into a house, he shall be buried, after he has been killed, in front of the site of the break-in.... If a robber is not caught, the city and the Elder shall replace for the person robbed everything they have lost.... If a man steels the underage son of another, he shall be killed.... If someone takes a wife but does not conclude a contract with her, then this woman is not his

> spouse.... If a man hires an ox for threshing, payment shall be one measure of grain. If a donkey is hired for threshing, payment shall be a half measure of grain....

Hardly a detail that Hammurabi has forgotten. His code regulates divorce, illness, property, inheritance law, the payment of day laborers, and much more, indeed, even the taking of hostages. At the end of his work, Hammurabi had the words chiseled into the pillar: "...In the days to come and for all time, let the king who rules this land observe the words of justice I have written on my monument."

Many legislators from other cultures did indeed use Hammurabi's code as a model in the course of human history. Today, his original stone pillar is kept in Paris in the Louvre.

It seems that those gods, the heavenly ones from another solar system, have repeatedly involved themselves in human development. And today? Where do we stand? Clearly they are involving themselves again. What future will that produce?

CHAPTER 5

WHAT NEXT?

At the end of the 1960s, a book was published that changed the world: *The Limits to Growth.*[1] Published under the umbrella of the Club of Rome, an affiliation of various scientists, the title became a number-one best-seller in all industrialized nations. The then UN Secretary-General, U. Thant, wrote an introduction uniquely in the history of the UN:

> I do not wish to seem overdramatic, but I can only conclude from the information that is available to me as Secretary-General, that the Members of the United Nations have perhaps ten years left in which to subordinate their ancient quarrels and launch a global partnership to curb the arms race, to improve the human environment, to defuse the population explosion, and to supply the required momentum to development efforts. If such a global partnership is not forged within the next decade, then I very

much fear that the problems I have mentioned will have reached such staggering proportions that they will be beyond our capacity to control.

Ten years after the publication of the book, our civilization would be in such a miserable state that the problems would be *beyond our capacity to control.* How did the UN Secretary-General come to make such a devastating statement? He referred to the thoroughly honest scientists of the Club of Rome, who had calculated the models of the future. These models were based on the data available at the time. They were all correct, but there was one factor that was very difficult to calculate: human inventiveness, intelligence, and creativity. Thus, *The Limits to Growth* became the first fear-inducing title. Every reasonable person had to be concerned about the state of the earth. Despite knowing about the gaps in their models, the authors wrote, "Given the many approximations and limitations of the world model, there is no point in dwelling glumly on the series of catastrophes it tends to generate." What catastrophes would be generated?

...there will be a hopeless shortage of land even before the year 2000 if population growth continues as today...

...with the current increase in consumption, most of the most important non-renewable raw materials today will be extremely expensive in 100 years, even with the most optimistic assumptions of newly discovered reserves, technical progress and the use of suitable replacement materials...

> ...such systemic behavior clearly tends to-
> wards exceeding the limits to growth and then
> collapsing...[2]

After the well-founded warnings of the Club of Rome, humans had forest decline hammered into them. First the forests, then humans was one headline. Then bark beetles would eat our trees and finally acid rain would do the rest.

With all these scenarios, I ask myself why we are still alive at all. After all, we have reached 2016 and are swimming in crude oil. The biological time bomb has not exploded. Yet the apocalyptic horror show continues to be promoted. No matter whether we have a rainy or a hot summer, human beings are at fault in either case. Billions of dollars turn into thin air in questionable funds. Silently (angrily?), the shaken populace pays up. After all, it wants to stop climate change. As if carbon dioxide had caused climate change in any past. To be clear: Thousands of years ago, our earth suffered repeated climate change. Quite clearly verifiable. But at that time, there were neither industrial chimneys nor car emissions, yet there was still climate change. How about other causes for the climate change we are currently suffering? In *The Limits to Growth* the scientists note, "Carbon dioxide dissolves very easily in water."[3] Completely forgotten?

Who actually has an interest in placing all of humanity in a state of fear? To tell people things that are not actually true? And even if just a few models are wrong, why is the world press not up in arms about it? Is the world to be prepared to hope for some kind of savior? What has happened to the intelligence of Homo sapiens sapiens, which increasingly floods world politics and increasing numbers of universities with scientific nonsense like the so-called "gender model"? Gender? Everyone has heard about it but few know what it is actually about. The word *gender* is used to designate the psychological sex of a person in contrast to their biological sex. Is there such a thing as a "psychological sex"? Yes. A man can feel themselves to be a woman and vice versa. The concept of "gender" was invented as long ago as 1985 at the UN World Conference on Women in Nairobi and framed in 1995 at the UN World Conference on Women in Beijing. Within the framework of equality between men and women, some women demanded a program to implement gender equality. Meanwhile, gender has grown into a proper world strategy. "Gender mainstreaming" is even one of the goals of the European Union. But a few fundamentally correct thoughts have turned into a feminist world dictate. There are hardly any scientists left who have the moral courage to stand up against gender. One exception is the German Professor Ulrich Kutschera of the Universities of Kassel and Stanford. In an interview with the German news magazine *Focus*, Kutschera described gender as an "irrational doctrine."[4] With gender all scientific facts of biology were denied. "The gender mainstreaming ideology comes from a radical feminist sect-like esotericism of the 1990s. It is devoid of any scientific basis."[5] The combative professor underpinned his analysis against gender with an outstanding factual book.[6]

What is supposed to be so wrong about gender? We are all made the same. There are only unisex people any longer.

The biological sex no longer counts for anything. Boys should actually be ashamed to have been born with a penis. The original idea for this nonsense comes from the American professor John Money (1921–2006). He already said in 1955 that all babies were born as gender-neutral unisex beings. In an experiment, he had one of two identical twin brothers, David and Brian Reimer, surgically reassigned as a woman. Although this perverse experiment was a total failure, it is still propagated by the gender supporters as evidence of the unisex idea. Brian committed suicide at the age of 36, David two years later.

Today, gender is taught at many universities. It is the same as evolutionary theory: Anyone who does not adhere to "gender" is excluded from the community of reasonable people. God as a male figure is no longer allowed. A court in Portland, Oregon has granted a person genderlessness. Jamie Shupe, born as a male, wanted to be neither a man nor a woman, neither mister nor ms., but MX Shupe. "Jamie Shupe is now MX Shupe, and MX Shupe is waiting for a new ID card in which it will not say male or female but 'non-binary'" writes the German news magazine *Der Spiegel*.[7] I suppose next there won't be any "rapist" or "stay-at-home." (Translator's note: Both are masculine nouns in German.) Either, after all, we are all gender-neutral.

"These Romans are crazy," was a catchphrase in Asterix. These people are crazy, we should say. And although millions of earth citizens worldwide, including no doubt many scientists, are of the same opinion as myself, hardly any of it gets out. What is wrong with our media? With our sharp and alert journalists? Have they all gone to sleep or is there a higher power somewhere that suppresses any critical questioning?

The problem lies in the poison that is ideologies. They have the same effect as dictatorial religions. And anyone who in a given geographical area thinks differently from what happens to be the ruling religion will be denigrated. Anything that is not left-wing thought is "populism," "misanthropic," and "regressive" for the Left. And anything that is not right-wing thought is a "betrayal of the nation," "hypocritical," and "mendacious" for the Right. No decent right-winger will attend an event of a left-wing politician and vice versa. The "dogmatists" reign supreme. Everyone wants to be "rational" and be with other rational people. Irrationality means exposing oneself to ridicule—and no one wants that. Now, and this is a truism, every newspaper, every magazine, every TV station has an owner. It may be a rich family, an individual person, a political grouping, a trade union, or the state. Everything belongs to someone. Each owner wants to belong to the rational people in their trade. If a journalist wanted to put something "irrational" into their paper, they wouldn't get it past their editor. If they did, they would soon be out of a job. We don't have to conjure up conspiracy theories to recognize this behavior of people. What is lacking is moral courage and anyone who has it is excluded. The same applies with regard to the puppet theatre of the so-called "broadcasting councils." What was that about the extraterrestrials from the future in the first chapter? All of them beautiful people with sparkling white teeth, soft kissable lips, and a delicate body. But no distinction between men and women could be identified.

In May 2016, 160 people came to a meeting at the Harvard Medical School in Boston for an exchange of views, which was originally meant to be kept secret. They discussed the question of the artificial human genome. Will we be able to produce humans with specific characteristics in the future? The question is ethically highly controversial because when humans can create specific humans they are playing at being god. And they will do so; at some point, just like the ETs have done.

On June 28, 2016, Jean-Claude Juncker, the president of the European Commission, gave a remarkable speech to the European Parliament. It was about the departure of Great Britain from the European Union—so-called BREXIT. Juncker showed his concern and said, "Make no mistake, those who are watching us from afar are concerned. I have met and listened to *several leaders from other planets.* They are very worried because they are wondering about the course the European Union will take. So we must reassure Europeans and those who are watching us from further away...."

The media interpreted Juncker's words "several leaders from other planets" as a translation error or slip of the tongue. Not so. Juncker gave his speech in French. The words *pays* (country) and *planète* (planet) are very different. Furthermore, the explanation of a slip of the tongue does not fit into the context of the text. (I speak French and do not need a translator.) Juncker continued, "...et ceux qui nous observe de plus loin," which means "and those who observe us from further away." Now, Mr. Juncker should be given the benefit of the doubt that he was tired and annoyed by some hecklers. The question must nevertheless be permitted: Is he aware of contact with extraterrestrials? Is it really due to tiredness that his brain no longer kept things apart? And what makes me personally sit up and pay attention: The whole passage was removed from the official text of the Juncker speech. Censorship. But why in the world would extraterrestrials be worried about the cohesion of Europe? Why would they remotely care about that? We can speculate. Presumably the ETs want to conclude their treaties with a united Earth. Europe is one piece of the puzzle. We must all be the same.

Irrespective of such curiosities, humans are moving in an irreversible direction prescribed by computer technology and the inevitable arrival of artificial intelligence (AI).

The meanwhile retired Professor Edward Fredkin (physicist, Boston University, MIT, and CALTECH) is convinced that the electrons whizzing around the atomic nucleus constantly exchanging information with other electrons are based on something like binary code. The whole universe, says Fredkin, is ruled by some program, just like in the model of god as a universal computer or god as a mathematical formula. "What is life?" asks Fredkin. "What is consciousness, what is thinking, memory, and those things?" Fredkin recognizes in our DNA, which is passed on from generation to generation, nothing other than digitally encoded information.[8] From the beginning, this information contains the answer to our development as a life form. Whether DNA turns into a plant (which one?) or an animal (which one?) is determined from the beginning. "The electron is nothing other than a part of the answer." Somewhere out there, Fredkin says, there exists a "machine-like thing"[9] that controls the laws of the universe.

This "machine-like thing" controls the extraterrestrials and they in turn control us. For years, brain researchers have repeatedly tried to pin down the miracle of God. Where does the power of faith come from? It should be possible to show it in our grey cells, after all. Scientific experiments in a new discipline, neurotheology, have shown God is located in the brain. "Those who are willing to engage in inner contemplation manage it. Those who lack faith will not be helped by a magnetic field either."[10] The desire for something divine produces sublime feelings in the brain. Yet God as a being cannot be found. "Looking for God in the brain is like opening up the television to find the newsreader."[11] The fact that the brain can produce an "elevated feeling" of God does not mean that "God as a being" can be found. Electrons speeding around the atomic nucleus and exchanging their information with other electrons are not measurable. And placing a whole brain under a scanning electron microscope is not technically feasible. But in order to experience the "elevated feeling" of being in connection with some being of "God" requires the desire to experience just such a feeling. What came first, the chicken or the egg? Where does the desire come from? Our brain is, after all, a product of DNA and the latter of the cell. This, in turn, consists of millions of atoms and the extraordinary electrons orbit each atom. The DNA is where the information is stored, which provides the data for the development of that precise form of life. *This information exists before any life form even begins to grow.*

The 21st century will be the century of the technology of consciousness. No one can dispute the evolution of computers; after all, they are becoming ever more sophisticated with each generation. Computers will grow into units that program themselves. One of the leading lights in the computer industry, Dr. Raymond Kurzweil, is convinced that by 2045 at the latest, artificial intelligence will make humans superfluous. He calls that "singularity." The artificial intelligence of the future would behave in such a way toward humans that we would not even notice how intelligent computers are. Humans would not be able to notice it in any case because they simply lack the intelligence. We would be too stupid for that.

Some prospect! If the future of human beings no longer consists of anything but artificial intelligence, why then are humans necessary at all? And why extraterrestrials? And why is it necessary for the human species to be influenced by extraterrestrials today if we will no longer exist in the year XYZ anyway? Will there perhaps be superfast computers communicating with one another, and doing so faster than the speed of light and from star to star without us knowing about it? Is artificial intelligence perhaps developing a language that is incomprehensible to us? Or will artificial intelligence in the future take human form again for some reason to multiply more easily?

In Greek mythology, Pandora was the first woman. The father of the gods, Zeus, gave her a box with the command to give the box to human beings, but the box must not be opened under any circumstances. Zeus of course knew that human curiosity would lead to Pandora's box being opened. We have long opened the box. This is the opinion of the Japanese billionaire and cybernetics pioneer Yoshiyuki Sankai. In an interview with the newspaper *Die Welt*, he asserted, "Development is already very advanced; learning, artificial intelligence is already in military use in a very advanced form...combat robots on four legs can climb up mountains, can carry biological and chemical weapons and select their targets autonomously..."[12] Yoshiyuki Sankai notes with some resignation that we humans were the sole living beings who could override natural selection. Correction, dear Mr. Yoshiyuki Sankai. Extraterrestrials have been doing that for a long time.

How did we conceive of the idea of artificial intelligence in the first place? The idea has been stalking through science-fiction literature since time immemorial, but it became official on April 17, 1990. That is when the American Dr. Marvin Lee Minsky (1927–2016), professor at the Massachusetts Institute of Technology, received the prize of the Science and Technology Foundation of Japan. He received it expressly for his concept of artificial intelligence. The prize was presented to him in the National Theater of Tokyo in the presence of the Japanese imperial couple. Marvin Minsky had started studying studied the abilities of our brain as a young man and had raised the question: If the brain is a kind of machine, and if consciousness only arises because electrons and neurons are whizzing about causing an effect, then it should be possible to bring about the same effect artificially. Here crucial differences between a brain and a computer very quickly became apparent. Our brain functions because about a hundred billion neurons exchange messengers between one another and create a cognitive system through these connections, the so-called synapses. Because each nerve cell can pass on hundreds of contacts, a neural network is created in the human brain of up to 100 billion connections. The crucial factor here is that these neurons function as a network while with a computer the commands are executed consecutively. This is the critical difference. The steps in the computer were programmed beforehand. Be it by humans or computers, AI, is irrelevant. The computer performs "calculations," even if at lightning speed. The brain, in contrast, has the "complete overview." How does that work? When our eyes see a mountain landscape or our grandmother, they know in an instant what it is. Our brain does not have to "do the calculation." We can also drive a car, pay attention to everything on the road, speak with our passenger, listen to music, analyze an unpleasant smell, admire the mountain landscape, and think about sex. We can do all of these things and a lot more simultaneously.

In his brochure "Auf dem weg zu intelligenten Systemen" ("On the Way to Intelligent Systems"), Professor Rolf Pfeifer of the Department of Informatics of the University of Zürich points to a paradox. A chess master, Dr. Pfeifer says, can remember about 50,000 moves that they can call up in seconds. The more a chess master knows, the faster the identification of moves. In a computer program, in contrast, the time for finding a specific move increases the more possible moves are entered. "Human memory behaves in exactly the opposite way.... The more it knows, the faster it can find specific information."[13] The phenomenon was known as the "expert paradox." Then, in March 2016, the British neuroscientist Denis Hassabis programmed a self-learning computer with the software AlphaGo. The game "Go" is considered to be incredibly complex. Thirty million moves were entered. And lo and behold, the computer beat the best Go player, the South Korean Lee Sedol. A total of five games were played. AlphaGo won four of them. Beforehand, the computer with its program had played innumerable times against itself and in doing so constantly reprogrammed and improved itself. That is called a learning artificial intelligence. Will we humans therefore soon be duped by AI? And are the ETs out there who influence our history and observe us nothing other than artificial intelligence?

It cannot be ruled out. Yet our brain is much more sophisticated than the program AlphaGo because each human being is unique—but each artificial intelligence is not. Excuse me? The human brain is constantly programmed from birth. That can be shown with an example.

Before birth, every infant lay in the pleasant warmth of the womb. Let us call what they experienced there "pleasure." No sooner born, and the baby begins to cry. It feels the opposite of "pleasure," that is, "unpleasure." The infant wants food, they scream. Equivalent to "unpleasure." The breast or bottle is given—equals "pleasure." The infant gripes, is tired, wants company; this corresponds to the feeling of "unpleasure." Then familiar faces appear, the child hears blah...blah...blah, they are stroked, have their nappies changed—equals "pleasure." A few years later, the child is taught what they are and are not allowed to do. The child has their own first experiences. They fall over, cut, or burn themselves. All of it "unpleasure." The parents teach them which of the neighbors are nice and which ones aren't. Pleasure/unpleasure. A few more years later. The child has started going to school. Every time they understand something or are praised, they register as "pleasure." The opposite—bad pupil—as "unpleasure." Puberty follows. The first discoveries relating to their own body. The fervor of love, the rage of jealousy. Harmony, the happiness of togetherness, disappointment, the pain of separation, and so on. Everything is stored in the brain as "pleasure" and "unpleasure."

Now these experiences relate to all of us. So are we all the same after all?

Ten people of the same age sit in the same cinema, breath the same air, see the same film. Among the 10 there is a couple in love, holding hands. Someone else is restless; something is bothering him. Another is constantly comparing the action with another film in her mind. One person likes the actors, another finds them silly. One is afraid of the end, the other cannot wait for it. The dialogue is terrible, one complains. The other person feels himself as the main protagonist in a heroic scene, and so on, ad infinitum.

The same applies to every human action. Twenty people experience the camp fire, smell the scent of the wood, see the thunderstorm coming, but each one registers the course of events differently, connects it with different memories. Fifty thousand people in a football stadium, 300 in church, 1,000 at a political event. All of them experience something in common: the stadium, the teams, the uniting political or religious idea. Despite the many commonalities, each one has different thoughts, emotions, memories. About a hundred billion neurons exchange messengers in the human brain and create an extraordinary cognitive system through their synapses. But because every nerve cell is known to pass on hundreds of contacts, the neural network comprises 100 trillion connections. That number is not nearly enough. All people experience their senses differently. The taste of charcoal, rosemary, nutmeg, or the feeling of a lover's skin is absorbed differently by each person. Stroking, pressure on a part of the body, a kick in the groin, or fist in the face are all different. Every human eye sees different things. The ears of a musician hear different details from mine. This makes each person unique; scientifically easy to prove. Eight billion people live on the globe, but not one has the same fingerprint as their neighbor. The same is true of the genetic code. Each person is distinctive. And this also makes clear that the constant attempts of clever political men to make us all the same will forever remain an illusion.

If we were all identical, no extraterrestrial intelligence would bother with us. Because each one would be the same as their neighbor, contact with a single human being would be sufficient. "Humanity" would not be of interest. But now we are units that multiply with pleasure. Sex means the greatest pleasure. Then we collect information for a lifetime and pass it on through electrons. *The ETs out there are dependent on our diversity.*

Artificial intelligence can program itself, can learn to solve highly complex mathematical tasks in fractions of a second. But it has no emotion. We may now design robots that start to cry when they see something sad. Or others that stroke patients. I can easily imagine kissing and copulating robots that look like humans, act like humans, and smell like them. But they have no "spirit." "There will never be spirit born from software. And that is not a question of technical development but an a priori impossibility," says David Gelernter, professor of computer science at Yale University in New Haven, Connecticut.[14] "Our spirit is not static, it changes constantly. Not just in the course of our life but even during a day."[15]

That is what comprises the uniqueness of each person. It is not just a matter of thoughts that a computer may be able to "reproduce"; it is a matter of the memories, feelings, emotions, words, and sounds that together comprise the "spirit." This "spirit" cannot be confined. Information can be. Have the extraterrestrials somewhere stored a piece of information for us, ready to be called up? Where would we have to look?

All large organizations have stores of their knowledge. Examples? In the Second World War, the Swiss blasted tunnels and large chambers into their mountains. Subterranean barracks and hospitals were built. Ammunition depots, sleeping quarters, ventilation shafts, and whole cable car systems were anchored in the granite. Today many of these caverns, which could resist a nuclear attack, have been rented to companies on a long-term basis. That is where the knowledge of the company concerned is stored.

All the world's seeds are stored in Norway's Spitsbergen: about one million seed samples from potatoes, rice, wheat, grasses, and maize to every conceivable flower and crop plant. The facility, called Doomsday Seed Vault, lies in the Arctic and guarantees secure cooling even in the event of a power failure.

The Mormon Church, with its headquarters in Salt Lake City, has for decades registered all available data of humanity. About four billion records such as first and last names, genealogical information, and family history of both sexes, and so on are stored in the so-called "Granite Mountain Records Vault." The Mormon Church does not seek to keep its register secret. Everyone can find out about their family history there.

The Church of Scientology operates a vast bunker system under the desert of New Mexico between Santa Fe and Amarillo, New Mexico, the Trementina Base. It contains 140 tons of books, writings, and steel tablets, as well as more than 2,000 titanium capsules with computer data. The point on the ground in the desert under which the mighty archive is stored is marked on the surface by a symbol that can only be seen from the air: two intersecting circles with a diamond in the center of each. Just like the pictures in the cornfields.

Documents of all kinds have been stored for centuries under the walls of the Vatican in Rome: the Archivo Segreto Vaticano, the secret Vatican archive. Alongside ancient writings from various countries, the records of the proceedings in the witch-hunts as well as of Papal policy during the Nazi period are stored here. And, of course, documents about the contact with extraterrestrials. Fatima says hello!

Where are the archives of the ETs? Are there any kind of extraterrestrial legacies on Earth? Enoch, who was instructed by the ETs thousands of years ago, told his son before his departure into space, "And now, my son Methuselah...I have revealed everything to you and given you the books which concern all these things. Preserve, my son Methuselah, the books from your father's hand and give them to the coming generations of this world." (Book of Enoch, Chapter 81:10. Now the Arab historian Ahmad Al-Makrizi (c. 1300 AD), who cites ancient Egyptian sources in his work *Hitat*, assures us that the Great Pyramid had been built *before the Flood*. By whom? By the same Enoch! And this Mr. Al-Makrizi is not making things up because he fastidiously lists all Enoch's forebears up to the patriarch Adam. He also writes that the pyramid contained "books about all secret sciences. Furthermore, the treasures of the stars...a mighty quantity...."[16]

In fact, ever more shafts and chambers have been located in and under the Great Pyramid in recent years using the most modern measuring techniques. None of these chambers can be entered. The chimneys leading to them are too narrow to crawl through. (Which throws a clear light on the planning engineers of the time, who did not exist at the time of Cheops.) I for my part would not be surprised if books from Enoch with the messages from the ETs were found in the chambers.

I have reported previously about Göbekli Tepe in southeastern Turkey, which is thought to be 11,500 years old.[17] I know from a reliable source that the place is at least 10 times bigger than generally published. Further excavations are deliberately not being undertaken. After all, something unexpected might come to light.

A similar thing applies with regard to Gunung Padang. It lies in Java, 50 kilometers southwest of the city of Cianjur and is said to be at least 14,000 years old. C14 dating of human bones found within the site even produced an age of 20,000 years.[18] No matter which age is correct, one way or another Gunung Padang would be older than the Great Pyramid near Cairo—at least according to the dating of Egyptology.

Gunung Padang lies 890 meters above sea level and consists of several hills with terraces, including some of the hard plutonic rock andesite (hardness 8 according to the Mohn scale). Then there are walls of many thousands of basalt columns.

Photos on pages 186–188: The misunderstood basalt structures of Nan Madol on the tiny island of Pohnpei (Caroline Islands). Photo credits: Erich von Daniken, Beatenberg/Schweiz

Photos on page 189–191: Basalt columns at the Gunung Padang site, Java. Photo credits: Ramon Zurcher, Archiv EvD, Beatenberg/Schweiz

Basalt path at the Gunung Padang site, Java.
Photo credit: Ramon Zurcher, Archiv EvD, Beatenberg/Schweiz

The site is reminiscent of Nan Madol on the island of Pohnpei in the Caroline Islands (Micronesia). Here too more than 100,000 basalt columns were used for building and no one to the present day knows by whom and for what purpose.[19] In Gunung Padang, there are a number of curiosities. Magnetic irregularities are registered and in certain spots the compass keeps spinning. Measurements using geoelectrics and georadar show spaces deep below the site. *Gunung Padang* means "Mountain of Light" in the local language, and the place has been a sacred heavenly site for the indigenous peoples for thousands of years. Who knows what messages will appear beneath it? "The whole thing is a time capsule," write the authors Vantari and Mumford in the magazine *Nexus*.[20]

Time capsules from the ETs, prepared thousands of years ago for us people of the present time? Why bother if they are here anyway and could inform us at first hand? With their messages from the past, they could prove to us eternal doubters and disbelievers: *It was us* who founded your civilization. *We* brought about the positive mutations in your evolution. *We* controlled development. Carefully—but steadily.

It is possible that writings will be discovered in an ancient structure that explain everything. It is possible also that the "time capsule" has been orbiting our Earth since Odin's time and is only waiting to be collected by the space-faring generation. It is possible, furthermore, that a "von Neumann probe" has been orbiting in our solar system for thousands of years. What are "von Neumann probes"?

Johann von Neumann (1903–1957) was a brilliant mathematician. He developed the idea of a miniature robot that can keep replicating itself. It works like this: In the search for a suitable planet, a small probe is sent into space. As soon as the machine has found an inhabited planet, it remains orbiting in the respective solar system but at the same time produces a copy of itself. The copy, in turn, continues its flight. When another inhabited planet is found, the process repeats itself. The probes reproduce themselves like cells. The time comes when there are millions of "von Neumann probes" flying around a galaxy. All of them collect data that they send home—wherever that may be. Are such extraterrestrial probes flying around our locality as well? On November 6, 1991, the astronomer Jim Scotti from Arizona's Kitt Peak Observatory discovered a small object in our solar system. It was given the designation "1991 VG." It was thought to be a mini asteroid and large telescopes were pointed at it. But the strange object out there reflected the sunlight in different colors. It had to be something artificial, probably a burnt-out rocket stage. Precise calculations of its trajectory produced the result that the alien object had already passed near the Earth in 1958 and 1972. In other words, before we started traveling in space. The Australian astronomer Duncan Steel asked the question as long ago as 1995 whether this might be an alien "von Neumann probe." We will receive an answer at the earliest in the summer of 2017 when the thing will go racing past us again.

We will very soon be able to document the visit of extraterrestrials also without probes and time capsules. Increasing numbers of curious formations keep appearing on the surface of Mars that do not quite fit into the picture of a natural explanation. Enthusiasts who spend months sifting through the official NASA pictures from Mars have found pyramid-like structures as well as rectangular obelisks reaching into the sky and triangular blocks with the same side lengths. In addition, the riddles surrounding the moons of Mars, Phobos and Deimos, have still not been solved. The NASA probe DAWN, which flew past the mini planet Ceres in the asteroid belt, provided curious images of a pyramid-like mountain with black and white scratches, shiny white spots, and rectangular and square formations. As with all information that could turn our worldview on its head, such evidence disappears very quickly from screens. The NASA photos are publicly accessible but revealing pictures keep dematerializing into a hole of non-existence.

An old guard is at work on Earth that is attempting to sweep all discoveries about ETs in our solar system under the carpet and make them appear ridiculous. A pointless exercise, my friends from the other side! Despite diligent censorship, such knowledge can no longer be stopped. The messages cannot be ignored. Pandora's box can no longer be closed.

The British astrobiologist Professor Milton Wainwright from the universities of Sheffield and Buckingham has discovered organic substances from space at a height of 40 kilometers. The particles definitely do not exist on Earth. "The organisms must come from space," he told the British newspaper *The Daily Mail.*[21] "We found evidence that the DNA is not from Earth. If our organisms came from Earth, they must be contaminated with DNA from earth and they are not."

Really such a report from the kitchen of a thoroughly honest scientist should have gone around the world as a sensation. It was rapidly stifled.

Mr. Nick Pope worked for the British defense ministry for 21 years. There he was responsible both for the secret UFO files and those that were subsequently released for public access. I have known Nick for many years and value not just his British humor but also his serious analyses. It is to him that I owe sight of the files of the British defense ministry entitled "Global Strategic Trends Out to 2045." The document is 172 pages long and alongside the military future also deals with other aspects.[22] Nick Pope says, "As things stand at present, computer knowledge doubles every three years. In 2023, certain computers will catch up with the human brain, and in 2045, they could be 100,000 times more effective.... Could true artificial intelligence be possible one day soon, with science fiction become science fact?"[23]

We human beings have grown up on our world. The evolutionists are right, but not completely. The Earth was never a closed system. Throughout its developmental history, there were always specific artificial mutations. It can be shown in the human genome—it can be shown in our traditions.

Now a study group at the ETH Zürich (Zurich University of Science and Technology) has found that data can be fed into the DNA and subsequently read without error. Stored for all eternity.

There is no point in trying to deflect humanity from the path of knowledge. The evidence that human beings have been influenced by extraterrestrials throughout history to the present day is becoming more compelling by the day. In the longer term, the anti ET lobby doesn't stand a chance in any case. The message also resides in the DNA. In each of us. And it is passed on from one generation to the next. We would do well to come to terms with the presence of ETs. Then the shock will be avoided.

POSTSCRIPT

Roger flinched as the flickering started again on the floor of his living room. Nothing had happened for three-and-a-half months. Roger tripped over a stool, slid on his knees, and stared in surprise at an algebraic formula floating above the floor. Agitatedly he phoned his son.

"Take a photo of the thing! Quickly, Dad, before it disappears!"

"Reminds me of the S-c-h-r-ö-d-i-n-g-e-r equation." Peter Zwicky said slowly.

"Of *what*?"

"Erwin Schrödinger, Austrian physicist. Lived from 1887 to 1961. He received the Nobel Prize for physics in 1933. About 1926, he presented an equation that is the foundation of quantum physics."

$$E = \frac{\mathbf{p}^2}{2m} + V(\mathbf{r}, t)$$

"And what does this equation prove?" Roger senior wanted to know.

"In principle, the Schrödinger equation is a wave equation. It shows the change of a state *over time* through its energy. Ever heard of Schrödinger's cat?"

"The cat which is simultaneously both alive and dead?"

"As a result of the Schrödinger equation, our colleague Max Tegmark proved the multiverse.[1] Everything is everywhere and can be simultaneously. Those there, 107 years in the future, who have sent us this message, are indicating that the future is always with us. No matter what we do rightly or wrongly today: *the future happens regardless.*"

NOTES

Chapter 2

1. Kean, Leslie. *UFOs: Generäle, Piloten und Regierungsvertreter brechen ihr Schweigen*. Rottenburg, 2012.

2. DVD from the International EvD Congress. Rottenburg 2015.

3. Kean, Leslie. *UFOs: Generäle, Piloten und Regierungsvertreter brechen ihr Schweigen*. Rottenburg, 2012.

4. Ibid.

5. Ibid.

6. "Alien Technology," *Ottawa Citizen*, Feb. 28, 2007.

7. Kean, Leslie. *UFOs: Generäle, Piloten und Regierungsvertreter brechen ihr Schweigen*. Rottenburg, 2012.

8. Mack, John. *Abductions—Human Encounters with Aliens*. New York, 1994.

9. *http://community.zeit.*
   deben-rich-directorvonlockheed-stunkworks.

10. *Sagenhafte Zeiten*, no. 2 (2016).

11. Alexander, John B. *UFOs, Mythen, Verschwörungen und Fakten.* Rottenburg, 2013.

12. von Däniken, Erich. *Götterdämmerung.* Rottenburg, 2009.

13. Stella, Claudio. *Kontakt mit E.T. Die gesellschaftlichen Voraussetzungen—die Folgen.* Berlin, 2009.

14. von Däniken, Erich. *Die Götter waren Astronauten.* München, 2001. (New edition Rottenburg, 2015.)

15. Yallop, David. *Im Namen Gottes?* Munich, 1988.

16. Ibid.

17. "Declaration of Principles Concerning Activities Following the Detection of Extraterrestrial Intelligence." International Institute of Space, April l989.

18. Stella, Claudio. *Kontakt mit E.T. Die gesellschaftlichen Voraussetzungen—die Folgen.* Berlin, 2009.

19. Ibid.

20. Ibid.

21. von Ludwiger, Illobrand. *Ergebnisse aus 40 Jahren UFO-Forschung.* Rottenburg, 2015.

22. Mack, E.J. *Abductions—Human Encounters with Aliens.* New York, 1994.

23. Ludwiger, von, Illobrand. *Ergebnisse aus 40 Jahren UFO-Forschung.*

24. Fiebag, J. *Kontakt—UFO-Entführungen in Deutschland,* Österreich *und der Schweiz.* Munich, 1994.

25. von Zitate, Ed Mitchel. *Sagenhafte Zeiten*, no. 2 (2016): Beatenberg/Switzerland.

26. von Ludwiger, Illobrand. *Ergebnisse aus 40 Jahren UFO-Forschung*. Rottenburg, 2015.

27. "Alien Technology," *Ottawa Citizen*, Feb. 28, 2007.

28. *http://community.zeit.de ben-rich-director von lockheed-stunkworks*

29. von Däniken, Erich. *Was ich seit Jahrzehnten verschwiegen habe*. Rottenburg, 2015.

30. Kean, Leslie. *UFOs: Generäle, Piloten und Regierungsvertreter brechen ihr Schweigen*. Rottenburg, 2012.

31. Pope, Nick. April 8, 2016 lecture at the UFO Conference in Eureka Springs, Ozark Mountains, United States.

32. Kean, Leslie. *UFOs: Generäle, Piloten und Regierungsvertreter brechen ihr Schweigen*. Rottenburg, 2012.

33. Stella, Claudio. *Kontakt mit E.T. Die gesellschaftlichen Voraussetzungen—die Folgen*. Berlin, 2009.

34. Ibid.

35. Kautsch, Emil. *Die Apokryphen und Pseudepigraphen des Alten Testaments*. Band II, Tübingen, 1900. Das Buch Henoch.

36. von Däniken, Erich. *Die Steinzeit war ganz anders*. Munich, 1991.

37. ———. *Habe ich mich geirrt?* Munich, 1991.

38. ———. *Was ist falsch im Maya-Land?* Rottenburg, 2011.

39. Hoesek, William, R. "Economica and the Fermi Paradox," *IBIS* 60 (2007).

40. Ibid.

41. von Däniken, Erich. *Die Steinzeit war ganz anders.* Munich, 1991.

42. Maeden, G.T. *The circles Effect and its Mysteries.* Bradford-on-Avon, 1989.

43. Jung, C.G. *Ein moderner Mythos. Von Dingen die am Himmel gesehen werden.* Volume 10 of the Collected Works. Olten, 1976.

44. Noyes, Ralph. *Die Kreise im Korn.* Munich, 1991.

45. Evans, Hilary. "Das Paradox der Getreidekreise," in *Die Kreise im Korn.* Munich, 1991.

46. Thomas, Andy. "Crop Circles of 2015. A Persistent Intrigue," in *NEXUS* 22, no. 6 (2015).

47. Haselhoff, Eltjo. "Sendung," *Ancient Aliens*, History-Channel, 8th series, 2015.

48. ———. *Opinions and comments: Dispersion of energies in worldwide crop formations.* Eindhoven/Netherlands, 2000.

49. Noyes, Ralph. *Die Kreise im Korn.* Munich, 1991.

50. Ibid.

51. Ibid.

52. Ibid.

53. Ibid.

54. Ibid.

55. Ibid.

56. Wilson, Terry. *The Secret History of Crop Circles.* Devon, 1998.

57. von Däniken, Erich. *Die Steinzeit war ganz anders.* Munich, 1991.

58. ———. *Der Mittelmeerraum und seine mysteriöse Vorzeit.* Rottenburg, 2012.

59. Lüschen, Geneiève. "Die Sonne im Blick," in *Neue Zürcher Zeitung,* March 19, 2006.

60. Lutz, Robert. "Bayrisches (Stonehenge), 3000 Jahre vor Stonehenge," in *Die Weltwoche,* Feb. 20, 1992.

61. Kulke, Ulli. "Am Anfang war die Revolution," in *Die Welt,* December 21, 2005.

62. Schulz, Mathias. "Der Kult der Sternenmagier," in *Der Spiegel* no. 48 (2002).

63. Salas, Robert. *Unidentified: The UFO Phenomenon.* Pompton Plains, N.J.: New Page Books, 2015.

Chapter 3

1. Miller, Stanley. "A Production of Amino Acids under Possible Primitive Earth Conditions," in *Science,* 117 no. 3046 (1953).

2. Monod, Jacques. *Zufall und Notwendigkeit.* Munich, 1975.

3. Eigen, Manfred. *Das Spiel—Naturgesetze steuern den Zufall.* Munich, 1975.

4. Monod, Jacques. *Zufall und Notwendigkeit.* Munich, 1975.

5. Charon, Jean, E. *Der Geist der Materie.* Vienna, 1979.

6. Coppedege, James. *Evolution—Possible or Impossible?* Grand Rapids, 1973.

7. Monod, Jacques. *Zufall und Notwendigkeit.* Munich, 1975.

8. Wilder-Smith, A.E. *Herkunft und Zukunft des Menschen.* Stuttgart, 1975.

9. ———. *Die Demission des wissenschaftlichen Materialismus*. Heerbrugg, 1976.

10. Vollmert, Bruno. *Das Molekül und das Leben*. Reinbeck, 1985.

11. Crick, F.H. and L.E. Orgel. "Directed Panspermia." *Icarus* no. 19 (1973).

12. Ibid.

13. Milton, S. and R. Lewin. "Is anyone out here?" *New Scientist*, August, 1973.

14. Hoyle, Fred and N.C. *Wickramashinge. Die Lebenswolke*. Frankfurt, 1979.

15. Crick, F. *Life Itself. Its Origin and Nature*. London, 1981.

16. Hoyle F. and N.C. Wickramashinge. *Evolution aus dem All*. Frankfurt, 1982.

17. Hoyle, Fred. *Das intelligente Universum*. Frankfurt, 1984.

18. Lahav, E. "Kam Adam aus dem Weltall?" *Die Welt* 25 no. 6 (1980).

19. Vollmert, B. *Schöpfung*. Freiburg, 1988.

20. Ibid.

21. Wickramashinge, N.C. *Die Entdeckung ausserirdischen Lebens*. DVD, KOPP-Verlag, Rottenburg, 2015.

22. Stadler, Beda, M. *Es gibt keine menschlichen Gene*. Bern/Göttingen, 1997.

23. "Auferstehung der Toten," *Die Welt*, May 23, 2008.

24. Grolle, Johan. "Das Wesen Des Lebens," *Der Spiegel*, 13 (2016).

25. Imhalsy, Patrick and Elisa Forster. "So arbeitet die Gen-Schere," *NZZ*, February 7, 2016.

26. "Lenkwaffe im Zellkern," *Der Spiegel*, no. 18 (2015).

27. Stadler, Beda, M. *Es gibt keine menschlichen Gene.* Bern/Göttingen, 1997.

28. Darwin, Charles. *Die Entstehung der Arten.* Stuttgart, 1974.

29. Schildknecht, H. "Die Bombardierkäfer und ihre Explosionschemie," *Angewandte Chemie,* no 73 (1961).

30. Wachmann, E. and Andere Laufkäfer. *Beobachtung und Lebensweise.* Augsburg, 1995.

31. Stadler, Beda, M. *Es gibt keine menschlichen Gene.* Bern/Göttingen, 1997.

32. "Durch Gen-Rutsch zum nackten Affen," in *Der Spiegel,* 18, Hamburg, 1975.

33. "DNA sequence and comparative analysis of chimpanzee chromosome 22," several authors in *Nature* no 429 (2004).

34. Ibid.

35. Sanides, Silvia. "Mensch, du Affe!" *Focus* no. 23 (2006).

36. Blech, Jürg. "Geliebter Affe," *Der Spiegel* 21 (2006).

37. Ibid.

38. Mühlemann, Olivier. "Wie LUCA, die Urzelle des Lebens, entstand." *UNI Press Bern* no. 15 (2013).

39. Vollmert, B. *Schöpfung.* Freiburg, 1988.

40. Nagel, Thomas. *Mind and Cosmos: Why the Materialist Neo-Darwinian Conception of Nature Is Almost Certainly False.* Oxford University, 2012.

41. *Welt Am Sonntag* no. 24 (2006).

42. Cremo M.A. and R. L. Thompson. *Verbotene Archäologie.* Rottenburg, 2006.

43. Ibid.

44. Kulke, Ulli. "Der neue Nachbar aus der Höhle," *Wams* no 13 (2010).

45. von Däniken, Erich. *Beweise*. Düsseldorf, 1977.

46. ———. *Was ich seit Jahrzehnten verschwiegen habe*. Rottenburg, 2015.

47. Schott, A. *Das Gilgamesch-Epos*. Stuttgart, 1977.

48. Karst, J. *Eusebius Werke, 5. Band, die Chronik*. Leipzig, 1911.

49. Schott, A. *Das Gilgamesch-Epos*. Stuttgart, 1977.

50. von Däniken, Erich. *Das unheilige Buch*. Rottenburg, 2014.

51. Burgard, Hermann. *Encheduanna—Geheime Offenbarungen*. Gross-Gerau, 2012.

52. ———. *Encheduanna. Verschlüsselt, verschollen, verkannt*. Gross-Gerau, 2014.

53. Burrows, Millar. *Mehr Klarheit* über *die Schriftrollen. Die Lamech-Rolle*. Munich, 1958.

54. "DNA sequence and comparative analysis of chimpanzee chromosome 22," several authors in *Nature* no 429 (2004).

55. *http://community.zeit.de/user/debatz/beitrag/2010/10/26/quotufos-sind-realquot-dr-ben-rich-director-von-lockheed-skunkworks*

56. von Däniken, Erich. *Was ich jahrzehntelang verschwiegen habe*. Rottenburg, 2015.

Chapter 4

1. Kohlenberg, Karl F. *Enträtselte Vorzeit*. Munich, 1970.

2. Grimal, O. *Mythen der Völker*, Volume I, Frankfurt, 1967.

3. Homer. *Die Odysse.* Translated by Wolfgang Schade-waldt. Zürich, 2001.

4. von Däniken, Erich. *Im Namen von Zeus.* Munich, 1999.

5. Ibid., 151.

6. Mooney, George, W. *The Argonautica of Apollonius Rhodius.* Dublin, 1912.

7. Schwab, Gustav. *Sagen des Klassischen Altertums.* Heidelberg, 1972.

8. Ibid.

9. Ibid.

10. von Diodor, Sizilien. *Geschichtsbibliothek, 2. Buch.* Translated by Dr. Adolf Wahrmund. Stuttgart, 1867.

11. Wollheim da Fonseca. *Mythologie des alten Indien.* Berlin, 1856.

12. Andersen, Johannes C. *Myths & Legends of the Polynesians.* Tokyo, 1969.

13. Grey, George. *Polynesian Mythology.* London, 1885.

14. Stair, J.B. *Old Samoa.* London, 1897,

15. Smith, Percy S. *Hawaiki: The Original Home of the Maori.* Wellington, 1921.

16. Grimble, Arthur. *A Pattern of Islands.* London, 1970.

17. Grimble, Rosemary. *Migrations, Myth and Magic from the Gilbert Islands.* London, 1972.

18. Capell, A. *Afterworlds Beliefs in the New Hebrides.* London, 1938.

19. Riesenfeld, A. *The Megalithic Culture of Melanesia.* Leiden, 1950.

20. Turner, J. *Nineteen Years in Polynesia.* London, 1861.

21. Andersen, Johannes, C. *Myths & Legends of the Polynesians.* Tokyo, 1969.

22. Kautzsch, Emil. *Die Apokryphen und Pseudepigraphen des Alten Testaments. Bd. II, Das Buch Henoch.* Tübingen, 1900.

23. Andersen, Johannes, C. *Myths & Legends of the Polynesians.* Tokyo, 1969.

24. Ibid.

25. Buck, Peter, H. *Vikings of the Pacific.* Chicago, 1972.

26. Handy, Craighill E.S. *The Native Culture in the Marquesas. Bishop-Museum Bulletin No. 9.* Honolulu, 1927.

27. Habeck, Reinhard. "Himmelsbote Mayual und der Kuhstall Gottes" in *Ancient Skies* 31 no. 3 (1997).

28. Burgard, Hermann: "Uruk: Wo vom Himmel herabgestiegen wird" in *Ancient Skies* 22 no. 3 (1998).

29. Heidel, A. *The Babylonian Genesis.* Chicago, 1942.

30. von Däniken, Erich: *Götterdämmerung.* Rottenburg, 2009.

31. Ramayana. *The war in Ceylon.* London. (No author or year.)

32. Laufer, Berthold. "The Prehistory of Aviation" in *Field Museum of Natural History. Anthropological Series. Vol XVIII No.1.* Chicago, 1928.

33. Ibid.

34. Brugsch, Heinrich.*Die Sage von der geflügelten Sonnenscheibe nach altägyptischen Quellen.* Göttingen, 1870.

35. Kebra Negest. *Die Herrlichkeit der Könige.* Edited by Carl Bezold. Volume 23, Section 1, Chapter 30. Munich, 1905.

36. Ibid., Chapter 58.

37. da Fonseca, Wollheim. *Mythologie des alten Indien.* Berlin, 1856.

38. Rybakow, B. *Heidentum im alten Russland.* Moscow, 1988.

39. Rostislav. "Hier stieg Perun herab" in *Sagenhafte Zeiten* 5 no. 4 (2003).

40. Desjardins, P. Le *Pérou avant la conquête Espagnol.* Paris, 1858.

41. Terneux. *Essai sur la théogonie Mexicaine.* Paris, 1840.

42. Simon, Pedro. *Noticias Historiales de las Conquistas de Tierra Firme en las Indias Occidentales.* Bogota, 1890.

43. Métraux, A. *Die Osterinsel.* Munich, 1957.

44. Feer, Léon. *Anales du Musée Guimet. Extraits du Kandjour.* Paris, 1883.

45. Freuchen, Peter. *Book of the Eskimos.* Greenwich, 1961.

46. Nansen, Fridtjof. *Auf Schneeschuhen durch Grönland.* 1891.

47. Beutler, Rudolf. "Plutarchos von Athen" in *Paulys Realenzyklopädie der klassischen Altertumswissenschaft. Volume XXI.* Stuttgart, 1951.

48. Heidel, A. *The Babylonian Genesis.* Chicago, 1942.

49. Schiefer, V.A. *Kalewala, das Nationalepos der Finnen.* Munich, 1922.

50. Sahagun, Bernardino. *Wahrsagerei, Himmelskunde und Kalender der alten Azteken.* Translated by Professor Dr. L. Schulze-Jena. Stuttgart, 1950.

51. Ibid.

52. von Däniken, Erich. *Der Tag an dem die Götter kamen.* Munich, 1999.

53. Kraamer, S.N. *Sumerian Mythology*. Philadelphia, 1944.

54. Kohlenberg, Karl, F. *Enträtselte Zukunft*. Munich, 1972.

55. Grimal, P. *Mythen der Völker*. Munich, 1967.

56. Gottschalk, H. *Lexikon der Mythologie*. 1996.

57. Grimal, P. *Mythen der Völker*. Munich, 1967.

58. Ibid.

59. Marx, Helma. *Der Buch der Mythen*. Cologne, 1999.

60. Risi, Armin. *Ihr seid Lichtwesen*. Zürich, 2013, p. 253.

61. von Däniken, Erich. *Das unheilige Buch*. Rottenburg, 2014, p. 11.

62. Preuss, Theodor K. *Monumentale vorgeschichtliche Kunst*. Göttingen, 1926.

63. Stöpel, Theodor. *Südamerikanische prähistorische Tempel und Gottheiten*. Frankfurt, 1912.

64. Waters, Frank. *Book of the Hopi*. New York, 1963.

65. Blumrich, J.F. *Kasskara und die sieben Welten*. Munich, 1985.

66. Rahner, Karl. *Herders Theologisches Lexikon, Volume I*. Freiburg, 1972.

67. Ibid.

68. Blumrich, J.F. *Da tat sich der Himmel auf. Die Raumschiffe des Propheten Ezechiel und ihre Bestätigung durch modernste Technik*. Düsseldorf, 1973.

69. ———. *The spaceships of Ezechiel*. Norwich, 1974.

70. Sassoon, George and Dale Rodney. *The Manna Machine*. London, 1978, p. 76–79.

71. Langbein, Walter-Jörg. *Als Eva noch eine Göttin war*. Gross-Gerau, 2015.

72. Biglino, Mauro. *Kamen die Götter aus dem Weltall?* Rottenburg, 2015.

73. Ibid.

74. Ibid.

75. Barüske, Heinz (ed). *Eskimo-Märchen*. Düsseldorf, 1969.

76. Hammitzsch, Horst (ed). *Japanische Volksmärchen*. Düsseldorf, 1964.

77. Ibid.

78. Brunner-Traut, E. *Altägyptische Märchen*. Düsseldorf, 1963.

79. Christensen, Arthur. *Persische Märchen*. Düsseldorf, 1958.

80. Gottschalk, H. *Lexikon der Mythologie*. 1996.

81. Grimal, P. *Mythen der Völker*. Munich, 1967.

82. Grömling,Willi. *Tibets altes Geheimnis. Gesar, ein Sohn des Himmels*. Gross-Gerau, 2005.

83. Marx, Helma. *Der Buch der Mythen*. Cologne, 1999.

84. Ibid.

85. Marriott, Alice and Rachlin. *Plains Indian Mythology*. New York, 1975.

86. Kisari, Mohan, Ganguli. *The Mahabharata*. Translated from the original Sanskrit text. Volume I and II. New Dehli, 2000.

87. Roy, Chandra Protap. *The Mahabharata. Drona Parva*. Calcutta, 1888.

88. Ibid.

89. von Däniken, Erich. *Habe ich mich geirrt?* Munich, 1991, p. 212.

90. Ludwig, A. *Abhandlungen* über *das Ramayana und die Beziehungen desselben zum Mahabharata*. Prague, 1894.

91. Jacobi, Hermann. *Das Ramayana*. Bonn, 1893.

92. Tessmann, Günter. *Die Bafia und die Kultur der Kamerun-Bantu*. Stuttgart, 1934.

93. Hübner, Paul. *Vom ersten Menschen wird erzählt*. Düsseldorf, 1969.

94. Bin Gorion, Micha Josef. *Die Sagen der Juden von der Urzeit*. Frankfurt, 1919.

95. Grömling, Willi. *Tibets altes Geheimnis. Gesar, ein Sohn des Himmels*. Gross-Gerau, 2005.

96. von Kremer, Alfred. *Über die Südarabische Sage*. Leipzig, 1866.

97. Turner, J. *Nineteen Years in Polynesia*. London, 1861.

98. Roy, Chandra Protap. *The Mahabharata. Drona Parva*. Calcutta, 1888.

99. Kautzsch, Emil. *Die Apokryphen und Pseudepigraphen des Alten Testaments. Bd. II, Das Buch Henoch*. Tübingen, 1900.

100. Diodor von Sizilien. *Geschichtsbibliothek, 2. Buch*. Translated by Dr. Adolf Wahrmund. Stuttgart, 1867.

101. Herodot. *Historien, Vol. II*. Munich, 1963.

102. Plato. *Apology, Crition*. Cambridge, 1917.

103. von Humboldt, Wilhelm. *Über das vergleichende Sprachstudium in Beziehung auf die verschiedenen Epochen der Sprachentwicklung*. Darmstadt, 1963.

104. Schott, A. *Das Gilgamesch-Epos*. Stuttgart, 1958.

105. Kohlenberg, Karl F. *Enträtselte Vorzeit*. Munich, 1970.

106. Frischauer, Paul. *Es steht geschrieben*. Zürich, 1967.

Chapter 5

1. Meadows, D.L. *Die Grenzen des Wachstums*. Stuttgart, 1972.

2. "Mx Schupe," in *Der Spiegel* no. 28 (2016).

3. Meadows, D.L. *Die Grenzen des Wachstums*. Stuttgart, 1972.

4. "Gender ist Nonsens!" in *Focus* no. 38 (2015).

5. Ibid.

6. Kutschera, Ulrich. *Das Gender Paradox*. Berlin, 2016.

7. "Mx Schupe," in *Der Spiegel* no. 28 (2016).

8. Wright, Robert. *Three Scientists and Their Gods*. New York, 1988.

9. Ibid.

10. Furger, Michael. "Gott im Kopf," in *NZZ am Sonntag* (December 21, 2014).

11. Ibid.

12. "Büchse der Roboter," in *Die Welt* (January 2, 2016).

13. Pfeifer, Rolf, Thomas Rothenfluh, and Zoltan Schreter. "Auf dem Weg zu intelligenten Systemen." Zürich, 1988.

14. "Die meisten Forscher begreifen nicht Ansatzweise," in *Focus* no. 10 (2016).

15. Gelernter, David. *Gezeiten des Geistes*. Frankfurt, 2016.

16. Al-Makrizi. *Das Pyramidenkapitel in Al-Makrizis Werk "Hitat."* Translated by Dr. Erich Graefe. Leipzig, 1911.

17. von Däniken, Erich. *Der Mittelmeerraum und seine mysteriöse Vorzeit*. Rottenburg, 2012.

18. Bachelard, Michael. "Digging for the truth at contoversial megalitic sides," *Sydney Morning Herald*, July 27, 2013.

19. von Däniken, Erich. *Aussaat und Kosmos*. Düsseldorf, 1972, p. 129.

20. Narada F. Vantari and Pratima Mumford-Sephton. "Rewriting Prehistory at Gunung Padang," in *Nexus* vol. 23 (May 2016).

21. "Dr. Milton Wainwright says he has found organisms 25 miles above Earth." *Daily Mail*, September 15, 2015.

22. Pope, Nick. "Terminator and X-Man: A Government Vision of the Future." (The document can be called up from Ministry of Defense (MoD), Development, Concepts and Doctrine Center (DCDC).

23. Ibid.

Postscript

1. Tegmark, Max. *Unser Mathematisches Universum*. Berlin, 2015.

INDEX

ABOUT THE
AUTHOR

Born on April 14th, 1935, in Zofingen, Switzerland, Erich von Däniken was educated at the College St. Michel in Fribourg, where he was already occupying his time with the study of ancient holy writings. While managing director of a Swiss 5-star hotel, he wrote his first book, *Chariots of the Gods*, which was an immediate best-seller in the United States, Germany, and later in 38 other countries. He won instant fame in the United States as a result of the television special *In Search of Ancient Astronauts*, which was based on that book. His other books, including the more recent *Twilight of the Gods* and *Odyssey of the Gods*, have been translated into 32 languages and have sold more than 63 million copies worldwide.

From his books, two full-length documentary films have been produced, *Chariots of the Gods* and *Messages of the Gods*. He is featured in the History Channel's extremely successful series *Ancient Aliens*, for which Giorgio A. Tsoukalos, of the Center for Ancient Astronaut Research and publisher of Legendary Times magazine, serves as consulting producer.

Of the more than 3,000 lectures that Erich von Däniken has given in 25 countries, more than 500 were presented at universities. Fluent in four languages, Erich von Däniken is an avid researcher and a compulsive traveler, averaging 100,000 miles each year to the most remote spots on the globe. This enables him to closely examine the phenomena about which he writes. Erich von Däniken is a member of the Swiss Writers Association, the German Writers Association, and the International PEN Club. He was awarded with an honorary doctorate degree by the La Universidad Boliviana. He received the Huesped Illustre award from the cities of Ica and Nazca in Peru. In Brazil he received the Lourenço Filho award in Gold and Platinum, and in Germany he was awarded with the Order of Cordon Bleu du Saint Esprit (together with the German astronaut Ulf Merbold). In 2004, he was awarded the Explorers Festival prize.

In 1998, Erich von Däniken cofounded the Archaeology, Astronautics, and SETI Research Society (AASRS), which publishes the English journal Legendary Times, reporting on the latest research in the paleo-SETI field. In 2003, he opened his "Mysteries of the World" theme park in Interlaken, Switzerland, which still fascinates visitors with his research into the various mysteries of the world, including paleo-SETI and the Ancient Astronaut Theory.

Today, Erich von Däniken lives in the small mountain village of Beatenberg in Switzerland (40 miles from Berne, above the city of Interlaken). He has been married to Elisabeth Skaja since 1960. He has one daughter, Cornelia (born 1963), and two grandchildren. Von Däniken is an amateur chef and a lover of Bordeaux wines.